Granada in Focus

DIRECCIÓN, SELECCIÓN Y MAQUETACIÓN
Miguel Román Vega

REDACCIÓN
José Fernández Echeverría

EDICIÓN, REALIZACIÓN Y FOTOGRAFÍA
Juan Agustín Núñez Guarde

FOTOMECÁNICA
Franacolor, S.A. Granada

SELECCIÓN DE COLOR
Juan Miguel García Sánchez

PELÍCULA ORIGINAL
Ektachrome 100 X EPZ 120 PROFESIONAL y
Ektachrome 64 X PLUS 120 de KODAK

REVELADO E-6:
Pablo Unica (Goyo Fotocolor)

IMPRESIÓN
Coopartgraf. Albolote (Granada)

FOTOCOMPOSICIÓN
Portada, S.L. Granada

© COPYRIGHT DEL TEXTO
Juan Mata

© COPYRIGHT
Edilux

DISTRIBUCIÓN
Edilux
C/ Albahaca, 1-5º F
18006-Granada. Tel. y Fax (958) 132245

DEP. LEGAL Gr. 1170-1992   ISBN 84-8782-66-0

Made in Spain

Granada in Focus

Text:
Juan Mata

Photography by
J. Agustín Núñez

Translated by
John Trout

Edilux

A city is always indifferent to the arrival of a young country boy; it scares him and stirs in him a vague sensation of insignificance and unworthiness. He has just been torn from the streets of his childhood with neither warning nor explanation and bundled into a taxi —a black car waiting at the door of what was his home, with the roof piled high with bags and baggage, surrounded by silent, curious neighbours— and been driven along a deserted road flanked by interminable olive groves, to a city which at that moment is nothing but a name. Granada; one of the eight provincial capitals of Andalucía according to his standard school encyclopaedia, where, if the night-time conversations of his elders were to be believed, every kind of specialist lives: kidney specialists, automobile specialists, procedural law specialists. It's a journey with no going back, which the village lad, his childhood drawing to a close, cannot yet conceive as being permanent. In the streets he has just left behind he was someone. In the city he is nobody. He is bereft of identity. He is an intruder, condemned to accept the future that is reserved for all emigrants even before they abandon their birthplace: to integrate without understanding, to banish the bewilderment from his eyes, to become part of the routine of the city and hope for better days.

At first the city is all tangled up and confusing. Conquering a city means learning to name it, to look at it as though it were being looked at for the first time, with innocent eyes, unclouded by custom, nostalgia or doubt. Every step taken through streets unplayed in as a child gives birth to a memory. Everything is to be admired because it is the fruit of wonder. One must learn to forget, to invade the territory of others, inch by inch, without help, without losing heart or giving in to dumb insensitivity, never passing up the chance for new discoveries. Cities do not present themselves ready made, they build themselves the more they are looked at. It is a patient exercise of deciphering that the newcomer has to undertake, without advice or warning or constraints, inventing the rules and the mistakes at the same time, free but also unguided. Like a watchmaker he separates the city into its tiny pieces and discovers the precise mechanism of deeds and rituals that its inhabitants repeat tirelessly: crossing themselves on passing the church of the patron saint; going to the square in front of the town hall on the day of the capitulation of the city to the Christians; eating salt loaves and dried cod on *St. Cecilio's Day*; wearing new clothes during *Corpus Christi*; climbing the streets of the Albaicín on the *Day of the Cross*; celebrating family saints' days in the local taverns. It involves a cabalistic apprenticeship in the interpretation of the city: learning the names of the shops where they sell the strongest shoes, and the cheapest toys; recognising the unmistakable characteristics of a loaf from Alfacar or of the genuine burnt-cream sponge cakes made in Santa Fé; knowing where the forbidden alleyways are to be found and where the most convenient places to arrange to meet someone are.

In the city of the recently arrived village boy there are no marble columns, no venerable cedars, no dignified windows. Only an accumulation of simple, hitherto unknown sensations: the rotting smell of the *River Darro*; the stalls selling quinces, haws and hackberries at the end of September; a strange accent on the tongues of the people; new voices heard at the barber's, on the buses, in the grocer's; the sweet taste of frothy cordials served in a tiny shop in the *Carrera de la Virgen* and the Italian ice-creams sold at *La Veneciana*; and also the stranger's new and disconcerting fear stemming from his irreversible uprooting and his solitude. That Granada of legend, which has astounded and seduced so many throughout the centuries, will reveal itself little by little, unhurriedly, imperceptibly. The *Alhambra* and the *Generalife* are at first a vast garden where a boy can stage races with boats made of conker-shell hulls and bay leaves for sails in the pools and streams and stone bannisters running with water, where fresh water is given to visitors from underground cisterns.

Later it becomes an excuse to air in front of the girls a knowledge gleaned scantily from books, which, while not leading to amorous conquests at least gives a personal, albeit useless, sense of satisfaction in not holding tedious conversations plagued with trivialities: there is nothing yet to presage the final enthusiasm, the serene admiration which will cause him to return again and again down the years, with no desire to discover, only to savour the pleasure of being there.

The *Carmen de los Mártires* is above all a spiritual and peaceful garden, the perfect refuge for contemplating in solitude a future from which failure and unhappiness are excluded: no one has told him yet about the Carmelite convent that used to stand in that domestic paradise, or that for six years the prior of this convent was *San Juan de la Cruz*, who in those very gardens conceived the verses of his "*Noche Oscura*". He will only begin to read this book with halting admiration a little later, encouraged by an old teacher of literature's reading the poems in class with moving passion.

The *Hospital Real* will be first and foremost a place of learning, a long, lofty lecture theatre in the old chapel, imbued with an ancient, clinging chill. In the presbytery the lecturer's dais and the screen for showing the slides in the history-of-art class are arranged stern and distant like an experimental-design film. Later he will come to find out that this inhospitable building is a magnificent model of progressive art, of transitional architecture between the Gothic and the Renaissance, an innovative institution to tend the sick, a lunatic asylum and refuge for wayfarers and the needy, the crippled, the syphilitic. Here, locked up in one of its cells, was a young, disillusioned Portuguese soldier called *Juan Ciudad*, who sold books beside the city gate, the *Puerta de Elvira*, and was thought to be raving mad by his contemporaries, who saw him in the streets decrying to heaven the infamy of his past life of sin. This Portuguese soldier later devoted his life to caring for the poor and was canonized *San Juan de Dios*, but his name to the newcomer is still only a sign on a busy street in the town centre.

Thus, inexorably, with the stealth and inevitability of an incurable blight, does the vast memory of the city invade his own. True conquest is an act of submission. You truly possess what lies outside you when you yourself have been absorbed into it. Only then can you say that the city belongs to you. The city is an empty scene into which the villager has unwittingly been introducing his life; places set apart by some emotion —a goodbye, a

conversation— until the strange city he arrived in years before has revealed itself to him, taken on meaning. The hostile territories of the initial years will be changed into oases in the memory: the dirt road that lead from his new house to his school, flanked by waste-ground which made do as a football pitch during the holidays; the basement of an amusement arcade where he played ping-pong on Saturday afternoons and where he came to know the kindly face of vice; the bar where he stole into young manhood in the company of his pals; the book shop where he bought his first novel for a hundred pesetas; the gardens where he lay in wait for the girl to go past, the first and unforgettable girl he fell in love with without knowing how; the cinemas and cafes crowded with people waiting for the film to begin: a host of small places made special by remembrance, gratitude and constancy.

Sometimes I climb up to the square of the church of *San Nicolás*, just to look, at nothing in particular, in the same way as I have done on innumerable occasions. It is a square conceived exclusively for the dominion of the eyes, where one goes at any time without any purpose in mind, because one's feet lead there without being asked to. I sit there beside old men wrapped up in thick, woollen dressing gowns and women knitting, their laps piled up with skeins of wool. Local residents with time on their hands, they share this communal vantage point with intruders who trudge up to gaze at the distant calm of the city, to escape the noises and nervous bustle that stalk the streets below. And that is enough. There I always come across the village boy who used to be me, sitting on the same bench, with the same bewildered eyes of the newcomer. Many years have passed me by since that first time, and so often have I climbed up to this square since then that seeing has become a casual affair, a vague custom. I don't know whether I should admit to loving that city spread out below the square; one is aware of loving a woman, a book, even an hourglass, but I don't know whether this emotion is applicable to a city, to all its nooks and crannies and all its inhabitants. One strolls along its streets, sits on the benches in its squares, walks into bars, visits palaces and churches and bumps into friends. Every one of these acts constitutes a kind of pleasure. We sometimes speak about our city with passion, we miss it desperately when we are far away. We are tied to it by an undeniable force. But I can't say what the true nature of that tie might be. Perhaps our passion is quite simply the habit of looking.

More important still than cities themselves are the marks that they leave in the minds and imagination of men. We know that the age-old prestige of some cities survives long after their decline, whilst others live with the stigma of indifference, which nobody, neither the tourist board nor local sales and promotion experts can remedy. There are cities whose name alone draws us to them without our knowing why, cities that arouse and inspire in us the irresistible desire to travel, and Granada is one of these. Others, on the other hand, we pass by quickly, furious if our route obliges us to cross them from one side to the other, wishing with all our hearts that there were a ringroad to skip this unbearable leg of the journey. Some cities we enter inadvertently, almost by accident. But there are those that we go to deliberately with the spirit of a pilgrim. This good fortune lies beyond the best intentions of the citizens themselves, it owes nothing to their industry or their character —it has been forged over the centuries and is as impossible to contrive intentionally as it is to foretell—. To discover its motives does nothing to help change the future. Noble cities of times gone by are today mediocre villages of whose past splendour nothing remains but their fame, some ruins and the odd tale. Others, no less famous, have been slowly but surely disfigured by war, greed and neglect. Of many contemporary cities, on the other hand, we know nothing; they carry on without being noticed, hidden by the veil of insignificance, which is surely a more devastating fate than fire or plague.

Every morning coaches carrying travellers from remote parts park outside the *Carthusian Monastery*. Some of them are emblazoned with badges representing the commonest stereotypes of paradise: the sun, palm trees, pristine beaches, brilliant blue seas. The signs on them are written in unpronounceable languages. Transparent stickers in their rear windows advertise their comforts: reclining seats, air conditioning, video, lavatories, a small bar. Tourists get down out of them. They make their way into the monastery close, walking docilely in ragged groups behind a red handkerchief held reluctantly aloft by the guide. They climb the stairway and shuffle into the precinct, the cloistered patio, redolent of myrtles, orange trees and cypresses. From there to the refectory, the chapter house, the cells, the chapels opening onto the nave. They file into the church and the sacristy — resplendent, opulent, adorned with marble carved with the skill and imagination that one would usually attribute to the palace of an Indian prince— and then the *Sancta Sanctorum* —sophisticated and oppressive, in whose dome heavenly paradise is represented as the Baroque artist saw it in his mind's eye. They stroke the marble columns —although notices warn them against it— and admire the mahogany chests of drawers inlaid with ivory and silver, which the lay brother *José Manuel Vázquez* laboured over for thirty years. They return to their coach. They have covered hundreds of kilometres with the sole aim of finding out, moved by the desire to see the face of a strange city.

Buses unload passengers from time to time alongside the monastery, mainly students who walk past the doorway without looking, taciturn, preoccupied with intangible problems that will have vanished by the morning's end. They climb up along the tracks worn out of the hillside beneath the walls of the monastery to the university faculties above. A pair of mules are tethered to a bush. The buses continue their route to *La Cartuja*, a working-class neighbourhood made wretched by unemployment and the disrepute that always attaches itself to places which breed failure, a neighbourhood which, in a time gone by made legendary and somewhat ridiculous by imperfect memories, had the privilege of sheltering clandestine trades-union leaders and left-wing, political militants. Passengers who stay on the bus, anonymous, expressionless faces glued to the windows, have passed this monastery innumerable times; they are not unaware of its name nor of its renown; they recognise its towers and its close, the epidermis of a concealed place which still keeps its secrets from them, inaccessible, though still a part of the city they live in. They are used to the foreign registration plates, the exotic tourists on the periphery of their lives, who come from abroad to penetrate the walled city, so close to them but so removed from their daily business. They observe them without curiosity or judgement, as though they were watching drizzle falling or the news on television.

Any city is a multitude of cities in one, some visible, some hidden. The everyday streets may be irrelevant and vulgar, like the streets in a silent village in the Arabian desert. We might stroll along them like outsiders, ignoring the signs that give them their uniqueness and personality. A city is a network of tracks, joining banks, hospitals, markets, offices and homes, and at the same time is an endless source of surprises: semicircular arches, bronze balustrades and weather vanes. In Granada innumerable cities live together, each unbeknown to and often vastly different from the other. An imaginary but insurmountable divide, strengthened by habit and laziness separates them. The city of the beggars is different from the city that the travelling salesman or the artist perceives; not everyone sees the same faces, not everyone distinguishes the same light; not everyone puts a common value on the objects around him. No one's eyes are quite the same as the next's. sometimes I hear someone talking about Granada and get the impression that he is speaking about a different city from the one I live in; he describes the ringing of bells that I have never heard, secluded nooks crowned by a niche and a lamp, passers-by whom I have never met and never shall; images of another city, amiable, remote, unknown. Cities exist because of our desire to see them. The story of our lives is the relationship we have with them, with those we have seen and those still unknown but whose very existence obsesses us. It is this which shows who we are and justifies our very being. We spend half our lives searching for the past, travelling roads that always lead to the bones of a Greek temple abandoned on a hillside assaulted by flies and cicadas, to a crumbling chapel whose walls are covered with paintings of tall unrecognisable figures, to villages on which the centuries have heaped dignity, poverty and solitude, or sometimes just to find out that a lugubrious Roman dungeon has been turned into a peaceful cloth warehouse, or a cloister has become a prosperous run for chickens and rabbits.

But the desire to see does not always imply costly enterprises and making journeys to remote islands. You can travel round the world and come back after many years untouched and empty, like the man who returns with his bags packed with silk cloth, porcelain figures and silver beads; with booty as the only news of his journey. The desire to see can be fulfilled without leaving the streets where one lives. Change is not necessarily synonymous with travel. It can be a way of observing the faithfulness or indifference with which one moves about cities, including even the cities where one has never been nor is likely to go, which contain the future that everyone has imagined for himself. We do not come from one place alone, not even the place where we were born, but from many places, sometimes imaginary, which we learn to live in, or to dream about, those places that make us as we are, that lend us a little more dignity. Or at least leave us a little less ignorant.

Many years after the trams have ceased to glide round the city you can still see the rails winding between the cobbles. I'm not sure whether their survival is due to mercy or to negligence. Many of their lengths have indeed been ripped up; others covered in asphalt. Between the cracks in some streets their metallic gleam shines through from place to place. Two carriages were saved from the scrapyard and stand as ornaments in the avenue *Paseo de la Bomba*, although they are now half-destroyed and lifeless. If you follow the track of the rails that have been left in peace you can reconstruct whole routes, intersections and stops. The old city limits are still there to be made out. It isn't difficult to imagine streets lined with posts with outstretched arms hung with overhead cables, streets dotted with pedestrian refuges, ringing to the sound of tram bells, the hiss of the moving trolleys, the screech of dry brakes in need of a squirt of oil. Memories of childhood tricks come back; leaving bottle caps on the rails for the tram wheels to flatten so that we could tie them onto the end of the string we jerked at to start our tops spinning. And not just bottle tops, coins as well, and nails of all sorts, and in fact any kind of metal object. And I remember those oh such slow rides to the other side of town over distances that our young eyes magnified until Granada was converted into a city of cinematographic proportions; artful passengers who got on and off while the tram was still moving. Memories which maybe are not all my own, which I have stolen from the movies, from books or even from other people's recollections, which shouldn't be rejected just for not being my own, because they are welded into the tram lines, because they are part of the memory of the city that I have accepted as my home.

From time to time the drills of workmen repairing the drains break into a tombstone, an earthenware jar, a mosaic. These are fragments of other towns which also called themselves Granada, over which this city that we know as Granada has grown; remains no longer used for the task they were made for, which mere chance has preserved camouflaged within the entrails of the present city, where they turn up as an involuntary testimony to the fate that always converts the modern into archaeology. Thanks to these insignificant objects, made with no intention to last, we know that we are treading where once there were basilicas, city walls, souks, roads, mosques, convents, theatres, prisons. And of course public baths, which were so abundant and popularly frequented in the days of the *Nasrid* emirs that *Andrea Navagero*, Venetian Ambassador to the court of *Charles V* and one of the first visitors to record his impressions during his stay in Granada, marvelled that the Arabs, and particularly the women, used to bathe in public, a pagan habit which would continue to astonish for years to come successive travellers who passed through the city and who commented in their chronicles about the extravagant custom the Arabs had of purifying themselves even in December, an observation which makes us suspect that these early Christian chroniclers, whether they were lawyers, clergymen or ambassadors, had little respect for water. Nowadays, when we walk into a bank we are entering at the same time a grain market that once stood on that site; we walk through a space occupied by tables, lamps, aggressively modern counters, a space which was taken up in past times by other tables, other lamps, other counters, albeit more roughly shaped, at which bargains were sealed, sales made and loans agreed upon; and other people walked from side to side, waited their turn impatiently and counted their money carefully, just as they do today. While we browse through the fish stalls in the market we are strolling through a courtyard lit with oil lamps where a Moslem family is celebrating the end of Ramadan and at the same time we are passing down the gallery of a cloister during matins. Under the old, recently demolished public market, the remains of an Augustine monastery upon which it was built have appeared, and beneath them the foundations of Moorish houses and tombs similar to those that were found under the *Triunfo Gardens*, which cover the old cemetery of *Sahl Ben Malik*. The present is just as fleeting as this account of the irretrievable obliteration of the market of *San Agustín*, the place where the heartbeat of the city was so clearly to be felt and which has accidentally become the brief chronicle of a city that will before long be invisible. In years to come someone will go down into an underground car park looking for his car without realising that he is also entering a Moslem house, a convent, and a marketplace he has never seen.

Hiroshima was devastated by an atomic bomb. Thousands of its citizens died and many more were disfigured. But along with the buildings the fragile vestiges upon which our identity rests also disappeared: portraits, documents, friends. The city was rebuilt and so as not to forget what the mutilated faces of the survivors looked like they had to be reconstructed with the traces of their features that remained in the memory. Everyone described what he remembered, described eyes, lips, a nose, according to his memory. Someone put it all together patiently and sketched in all the features described, then finally drew a face that probably was not a reliable work of memory at all but of desire. Our memory is selective and fragmentary. Just as the remains of the Granadas that preceded ours are jumbled up in the rubble hidden under the pavements and in the objects kept in glass cases in museums. They are scarce and fragile but we can reconstruct from them an earthenware pitcher and imagine a corner, a home, the daily routine of going to the local well, a conversation, a piece of news, something that has happened on the other side of the mountain, the outbreak of war. A hundred years of history are written down in a shard of baked clay. Until recently in *calle Hileras* there was a textile business called *La Isla de Cuba*. Inside it had a dome covered in brightly coloured, Baroque, alfresco paintings representing abundance and prosperity, like those on the tops of Havana cigar boxes. This shop formed part of a group of businesses —some of which still survive— which boasted names of old places overseas: *Puerto Rico, Las Colonias, Las Américas* and so on, as if to prolong the ancient empire in the lettering of the commercial signboards. In the city, if we look, we can also come across the plaques of vanished institutes of learning, signs advertising hostels which last shut their doors who knows how long ago, the names of streets that no longer exist, torn posters advertising performances years after they have been and gone. They are the jetsam of the wreckage of old towns. These are the remains of all the cities with the name of Granada that have followed one upon the other throughout the centuries.

Old chronicles, ancient plans of Granada, the sketches of travellers who nosed around its streets, all bear witness to the existence of a dozen bridges that crossed the *River Darro* from where it flows into the city to where it finally joins up with the *River Genil*. Some of these bridges survived to appear in daguerreotypes. Today only four are still standing; of the rest hardly their memory remains. They were gradually demolished as the *Darro* was covered over. The memory of one of them, the last but one before the *Genil*, is preserved in the name of a street, *Puente de Castañeda*, with more unshakeable loyalty than that of the stones its arch was built of. Street names are entrusted with the task of safeguarding the memory of the city. It is a mission to which we often pay scant regard. Streets are dignified by their names. Names should rise above the grey functionality given to them by ordinal numbers, as ridiculous as the uniformity with which lazy municipal mindlessness often inflicts on all the streets of one neighbourhood, dubbing them with the names of bullfighters or birds or mythological characters, names which could easily be imposed on the streets of any quarter in any town in any part of the world, names which pay no heed to the geography of the site, to the streets that criss-crossed it, to the trades that went on and things that happened there to give them their identity and a place in our memories. These are sterile solutions, as rough and ready and ephemeral as renaming streets in honour of some personality of the day who it seems politic at that moment to honour. In time the old names always reemerge. *El Camino de Ronda* was once —and who remembers today— pompously called *Avenida del Almirante Carrero Blanco* and *calle Mesones* boasted for a while the name of the poet *José Ruiz Zorrilla*. The street known as *calle Carcel Baja*, on the other hand, under the cobbles of which must lie the foundations of the Italian commercial centre, the so-called *Alhóndiga de los Genoveses*, which flourished in the Granada of the *Nasrid* dynasty, only to be converted by the Catholic Monarchs into a prison, continues to show where this public gaol stood until its demolition at the end of the nineteenth century; just as *calle Carcel Alta* not far away, betrays the site of the prison belonging to the *Royal Chancellery*. Further from the beaten track, the narrow *cuesta del Pescado* reminds us that here was the old city gate *Bib Lacha*, which after the conquest became known as *Fish Gate* because it was where the fishmongers coming up from the coast sold off their catch; *plaza de los Lobos* was where the hunters displayed in public the wolves they had caught in the surrounding mountains in the days before their extinction.

Street signs essentially enable one to cross the city without getting lost, but they are also a constant reminder that one is passing through other cities that were there before, invisible cities whose streets were lined with public wash houses, old soap factories and sheds where hemp was beaten, gates in the city wall, water channels where dyers washed their silk and inns to cater for hungry travellers and locals alike. Looking at street signs one feels the secret emotion of a photographer in his darkroom who puts the paper into his developing tank and watches how vague silhouettes begin to appear on its white surface and slowly take shape and become recognisable images of figures and views of a shadowy and forgotten city; the seat where the magistrates of the *Catholic Monarchs* meted out justice before they were housed in the *Royal Chancellery*, and the spouts where the irrigation

channels of the *River Darro* spurted out, and the corners where sandal makers, basket weavers, cloth shearers, damask workers and sewers of wine skins plied their trades, as though they were the lines on the face of an industrious city of artisans; and the sites of the flour mills turned by the water rushing along the channel of the *Cadí*, and the ruins of palaces and convents and the fate of their owners, and also the names of locals who have deserved to be remembered by their town, and the customs that marked the very personality of this city.

Granada is a city whose very life depends upon words. At times an event, an anecdote, a character sums up in one expression what the sediment of many fleeting days has taken to build up. Part of a past which would otherwise be condemned to disappear survives in words, is rendered accessible and of common tender, swapped among its habitants as though they were passwords. Preserved with the same jealousy with which the *Sephardim* have handed down the language they spoke five centuries ago, the most valuable heirloom that they managed to steal away with them when they were dispersed, and which they still hold onto, diaphanous and fragile, intact among so many hostile languages, like a welcome refuge, a clear sign of their identity along with the keys to the houses they had to abandon

when they were expelled, keys which no longer fit any lock, which open no door, but which are still an unrefutable tie with the land they left. Not with any country or town in particular, but with a place idealised by separation and nostalgia. Words perpetuate what people tend to forget. Still today, many years after its closure, many older citizens continue to get off the bus at a ghost stop, that of the *Americano*, the name of an erstwhile, much frequented café at the end of the *Gran Vía*; the *Puente Verde* continues to be called so although nothing about the modern stone construction bears any resemblance to the ancient, green, wooden bridge that used to cross the river at that point; the lower part of *Puerta Real* is still referred to as *el Embovedado* as though the days and nights since the river *River Darro* was covered over in 1884 had never been. These familiar references will be used less and less frequently though, until they finally die out, just like so many that used to express the life of the city.

Walls often serve as the pages of a journal where the citizens record their protests - "No one has the right to judge my conscience"; "No to military service!"; "From defeat to defeat to the final victory" —testimonies to their anger— "Castration for rapists!" —outpourings of love— "Mario loves Monica". Frequent are the challenges, threats, vindications of personal tastes. It is the public jotter, the city created with a spray can, multifaceted and transitory.

Elsewhere the words are carved into marble tablets and brief allusions to the lives of eminent persons are scattered over the walls of the town, marking the spots where patriots were executed during the War of Independence, the headquarters of "The Most Worthy Economic Society of Friends of the Country", all of which we should know nothing about were it not for these inscriptions. Most of the plaques still evident today were put up in the nineteenth century; it is a mode of homage that has fallen into disuse. The tablet in *calle Párraga*, dating from 1922 and indicating the guest house where *Théophile Gautier* lodged during his stay in Granada, has been replaced by a cheap modern wall tile which relates, with greater enthusiasm than accuracy, that, "In this street lived the author of *"Viaje en España"*. In neighbouring *calle Gracia* there is another tablet, made illegible by grime and the passing years, which tells us that in the house which it is stuck to, the façade covered in almost completely faded paintings, *Eugenia Guzmán Portocarrero* was born, later to become wife to *Napoleon III* and *Empress of France*. Today the name over a ground-floor shop selling stockings, lingerie and lace, *Eugenia de Montijo*, is all that remains to remind us of the branch of the family who used to live there.

It is a common fate of the now scarce wall plaques scattered around the city that they should be hanging precariously onto the outside of some squalid building, blackened and disfigured by filth and neglect. Just such a one is that put up in 1870 on the house in *calle Aguila* to mark where the young *Mariana Pineda* lived and was arrested. Tablets like these are unwitting reminders of the wilful way in which we neglect our past, of the ordinary Granada, which is kept alive only by talking, listening and telling tales about the city, and by reading inscriptions on its walls.

Of the many cities called Granada I find the one preserved in old sepia photographs the most disturbing. It is a city that has gone now but which can still be recognised in some street corners and the odd façade of the Granada of today. Confronted with these old prints I feel the same uneasiness as I do before pictures of my parents when they were young. It is hard for me to come to terms with a past that they belonged to but I was not around in. It gives me a shiver to look at their features and foresee my own in them. It is like looking at a portrait of yourself painted before you were born. Staring at these photos the frontiers of time seem to dissolve and I begin to think I am living in a city where different ages coexist: one, the city

portrayed in the photographs, inhabited by young, vibrant men and women; and the other, the city that surrounds me, identical in many ways to the city in the photographs, where I can see the same faces now turned weary and sceptical. It is a way of peering into the past with the same ease as that with which we look into the mirror every morning, a mirror that gives us back the face of our predecessors. In these old prints we can see a city that was there before we were, but a city that already unknowingly contained us. We can see the water-sellers' donkeys with their panniers loaded with pitchers filled at the spring of *El Avellano*, ancient merry-go-rounds at the fairground during *Corpus Christi*, ice-cream vendors with little roulette wheels strung on their backs to tempt the kids to double or quits, young seamstresses lugging huge wicker baskets brimming with white linen, local policemen in their long Muscovite overcoats and London-bobby helmets. I can see them standing in the same places as I pass by every day, modern streets blocked with traffic and crowded with hoardings advertising EXPO '92. But they are older and worn with time now. This temporary spontaneity, the proof that you share the same space that belonged to people who lived decades before, is what makes these old sepia photographs so enigmatic. We still dig up vestiges and fragments, testimonies of other Granadas that once existed but we have never seen, but the city photographed earlier

this century is a city which, although it no longer exists, continues to live amongst us, an old man ageing at our side, mute and indifferent.

For older people these black and white photographs narrate the tale of their past. The insignificant, everyday events which they themselves have witnessed; a flock of goats crossing *Puerta Real*, a row of mule carts along the *Gran Vía*, a fair on the esplanade where a supermarket now stands, all take on unusual importance. The sugar-cane sellers, the beggars, the charlatans and quacks temporarily desert their anonymity and acquire a name and address to become the protagonists of some tale or anecdote. Their memories add to the infinite, apocryphal history of the city. For an instant, within a tiny confine, photograph, history and narrative —the weapons devised by man to counter death— are united and conspire together to reconstruct the city held captive within their pupils. A part of the old city is imprisoned within their eyes and destined to disappear with them. The older inhabitants miss the flocks of goats, the carts and the fairs on the esplanade now that none of them remain. Today they appreciate the things they considered backward when they were young because that city knew them when they were filled with dreams, whilst this one only grants them the possibility of nostalgia. The infinite sum of this nostalgia and these unfulfilled desires bears the name Granada. When I hear the old ones reminiscing and telling stories of days gone by, the Granada that I know becomes frail and vulnerable. I become conscious that the things which surround me will disappear; a few will survive a while longer before my eyes and those of my contemporaries, while another city, also called Granada, will gradually take its place. It disturbs me to know that in a few years time in some art gallery photographs of the face of today's city are waiting for me, a face I shall recognise as that of the city where my still unfulfilled desires were nurtured. For those of us who never knew this Granada of not long ago these old photographic prints have been handed down to us as a bequest. As I look at what the eyes of the photographer saw his vision becomes my own. My experience is widened with memories not of my own making, events I haven't lived through, with people I have never even met. The city that I believe I know is the Granada which I have looked at throughout my life, but these photographs make me an unwitting debtor to other eyes, other ways of seeing, and they incite me to share with a stranger an unexpected, unsolicited experience.

In one of these photographs there is a group of men and children standing on a winter's day in the middle of a square in the dying years of the nineteenth century. There are nine of them, all but one wearing a hat or cap; three of them are holding enormous, black umbrellas over their heads, while two others keep theirs closed; perhaps it is raining at that moment; the ground and the trees are covered with snow. They seem neither surprised nor upset, nor apprehensive, they are simply fixed, as though caught in an instant without anxiety or curiosity. Their earnest composure is grave and timeless. They observe the mysterious apparatus which the photographer is handling in front of them, seemingly unaware that they are the central figures, as if photography is no concern of theirs. The intensity of their gaze has not been corrupted by television and advertising. In old photographs I am not interested in the slightly silly, antiquated costumes nor the extravagant adornments, I'm not lured by the particular events that inspired them: the stalactites hanging from a public fountain in a sudden, almost arctic winter; the water-melon stalls in *plaza del Campillo*, nor the long, solemn, crowded processions of the *Virgen de las Angustias*; it is the posture of the passers-by that grips me, their way of looking and holding themselves. I don't care so much about the old physiognomy of the city as the anonymous people who inhabited it and their unconscious and posthumous victory over oblivion. I find it alluring to come face to face silently and shamelessly with another

man's gaze. I am aware that I live in the same city as these unknown passers-by, that I have sauntered along the same streets, have entered places they too have been in; these things make me resemble them to some extent. The look in their eyes, however, possesses a quality which makes them different from me: they see a city I shall never see, that no one will ever see again. They were the enzyme which developed the city I live in. I look at them avoiding all feelings of pity, although I know that some years after that photograph was taken a devastating war was to begin in Europe, followed by another twenty-five years later; that soon halls would open in the cities to show the fantastic invention of "cinematography"; that some of them would learn the words of *Celia Gámez's* songs by heart; others would move to inhospitable regions in the north in search of work; a military dictatorship would take over and then a republic, followed by a civil war in which some of the children in the square in the photographs would be killed; that the fountains in the city would be moved from one place to another, new streets would be opened up and tall, characterless buildings would be erected over the ruins of the houses seen in the photographs. I live now in the city into which they projected their future; they are still in the city I never knew, the Granada which at that time already contained elements of my present.

Unfortunately few and far between, book shops are places you can wander into with no real aim in mind and no curb on your time, places where you don't have to eat or drink anything or pay at the door. To find shelter in a book shop on a rainy day is a small, gratuitous, wilfully pointless pleasure. If the rain falls in a light drizzle the pleasure is keener still, as time seems to pass more slowly, better suited to an idle mood. Instead of searching for any book in particular the best thing is to turn your search into a voyage of discovery. All books then seem promising and delightful, the signs of a happy meeting guided solely by chance. The contrast between the inclement world outside and the calm of the glass-windowed womb you have sought refuge in gives you a wonderfully cosy sensation. Whiling away rainy afternoons in book shops. I have learnt that Granada is the name of a city invented by literature. Innumerable books speak of her. Each of these describe in detail one special Granada, unlike any other known city, a Granada of peaceful, permanently blue skies, old buildings dignified by the centuries. Since ancient times it has been exalted for its poetry. In these books, places are described which have all the qualities of fictitious scenes; their inhabitants resemble the characters in a novel. Maps have been drawn up of this literary city, and it even has an official street guide, identical to those of the city I live in, and although the similarities between one and the other are striking, the city I stroll through every day seems to me to be an imperfect copy of the Granada that lives in those books. The street on the other side of the book-shop window appears to be the creation of a writer lacking in imagination.

In 1845, twelve years after leaving the Spain he had lived in for over three years, *Richard Ford*, an English gentleman educated at Trinity College, Oxford, who took great pleasure in strolling around the streets of Andalucía dressed as a stable hand, published a memorable guide intended to satisfy the curiosity of would-be British travellers. It was an extraordinary success. Hundreds of copies were sold and the critics praised the literary quality of the work. Since then it has been claimed that an image of Spain was firmly engraved on the minds of *Richard Ford's* fellow countrymen which still endures today. The main purpose of the guide was to advise potential travellers, set them on the right track, teach them to open their eyes to "Spanish matters", its history, antiquities, legends, traditions, hostelry, and gastronomy. Nevertheless, it's title, "*Manual for Travellers through Spain and Readers at Home*", also seemed to anticipate the existence of a reticent, sedentary reader, who derived little satisfaction from travelling and who could encounter in the book an opportunity to reach the limits of Europe without crossing the frontiers of his own library. I am sure that *Richard Ford* was aware that in a book even the most detailed chronicle of a journey becomes transformed into a fascinating tale of the fantastic. The memory retains images of a city that words destroy. When we describe a city we are in fact inventing it. The past must needs be legendary. The city that one sees is not to be found in the words that describe it. For each and every reader words conjure up different, often contradictory worlds.

Granada is the name of an imaginary city to be found in the pages of books. In the archives of *Granada Guild Hall* a record exists of a petition entered by a visionary foreign car mechanic to excavate the hill of the *Alhambra* itself. He vouched that he knew where the legendary treasure was buried, hidden by the *Nasrid* kings before they retreated from Granada. Whenever he got the chance he would spout his arguments with apostolic zeal and, as though he had just compiled an inventory, would describe in great detail the magnitude of the hidden wealth: diadems of pearls, strings of rubies, shields and swords of the purest gold, china porcelain and enamels, brocades and glassware from Damascus —an unlikely catalogue, filched no doubt from the pages of some romance, and yet to which he lent the same credence as though it were an official inventory from the Ministry of the Exchequer. On

several occasions he came to Granada accompanied by a dowser who, in accordance with the assertions of the clairvoyant mechanic, succeeded in determining the exact site of the missing treasure. The local authorities turned his petition down, presumably considering it to be work of a joker or a lunatic, but this rejection did nothing to sway his convictions and his fantasy still ties him firmly to Granada, a bond more resistant than any granted by a birth certificate because it was born of desire and not chance. Perhaps the true attribute of cities which endure time is their ability to instil such inordinate fantasies in men. *Agustín Lara* wrote a famous song dedicated to Granada without ever having set foot in the town. Myths are more tenacious than reality. In tourist brochures and travel books the Mediterranean is still blue and transparent, bordered by serene, immaculately whitewashed villages, and India has neither beggars nor suffering, only tall pagodas encompassed by jungle where monkeys and elephants sport and where luxury has an inoffensive, ritual prestige. Granada is the name of a city made splendid by fiction.

Romantic literature has contrived an image of an oriental and courtly Granada tormented by bloody dynastic battles, and has populated it with sensual captive princesses, cruel and covetous nobles and forbidden loves, and it is the traces of this Granada that visitors still look for. The mythical Granada has so influenced the imagination of readers that even today invention clouds their eyes. Some guides tell tourists that the rust stains in the marble around the fountain in the *Sala de los Abencerrajes* in the *Alhambra* are traces of blood spilt by a group of valiant princes as they were treacherously cut down in a last desperate stand to defend their lineage. But this need not shock us; in fact what the guides are describing is only the Granada that already lives in people's imagination. Until only a few years ago there was a photographer's studio near the *Palace of Charles V* where young visitors would dress up in jellabas and turbans, recline on small cushions similar to those they imagined the original *Nasrid* sultans must have used, and have their photographs taken in front of a screen depicting one of the rooms of the *Alhambra*. This photograph represented for them the most meaningful record of their recent visit to the Moorish Palace. Cities are founded necessarily upon elegant lies. Another popular invention, and one that is no less widespread than the myth of its orientalism, is that of a humanistic, cultured and tolerant Granada, favoured by the Graces, a city of rare sensitivity, which is instilled in all those who are born or live there and which has begot artists and renowned intellectuals since the dawn of its history. These conceits are brandished as arguments for proclaiming the city to be the "Cultural Capital of Andalucía". More recent and less ambitious generations have fostered the illusion of a noisy, Arcadian night life, which turns the city into a fertile oasis of bars and pubs where happiness is a although facile privilege within everyone's reach, a lavish Granada that oral tradition will turn into a minor, rather domestic myth, if by-laws and angry neighbours do not prevent it. They are all the essential distortions of reality that create and strengthen the imaginary cities which live together under the name of Granada. The city one sees contains all the different cities of one's desires. Falsehoods are the literary face of desire.

When colonizers first set foot in the Indies, their imaginations fired by stories of chivalry, they desperately searched those unexplored lands for the marvels promised by the books they had read. They were pursuing a chimera, and the continent, which in truth was no less fantastic than the one invented by writers, seemed to them no more than an untameable world of savages, a breeder of mysterious and deadly fevers. Illusion has always been more powerful than reality. Every day visitors arrive in Granada with their eyes already tainted by the visions of others, confused by second-hand praise. In the homely, humdrum city that welcomes them, with its impersonal buildings and streets choked with traffic, where rubbish lies strewn about, beggars abound and paper-handkerchief sellers accost drivers at traffic lights, they try to find the city of their imagination. But this is another city, no less real although somewhat less perfect than the one described in the books. Within every city there exist two dissimilar but complementary cities. This is also true of Granada: the streets where our lives evolve reveal the solid achievements of its inhabitants, clumsy, contradictory and inconclusive, whereas in the streets of the other Granada, the one we come across in the unsoiled pages of books, their inner desires are expressed, harmonious and judicious. This is why guidebooks and travellers tales exist, so that visitors may recognize the city of their desires in the imperfect city erected by men.

At the junction of *calle Colcha* and *calle Pavaneras* there stands a bronze statue of *Yehuda Ibn Tibon*, a Jew born in Granada in the last half of the eleventh century. He was an eminent doctor, philosopher and translator and, more because of a lack of interest than the passing centuries, he has become a stranger to his own city. There he stands, erect, in prophetic pose, a manuscript held aloft in his raised left hand, as though addressing a huge crowd who await his exhortation to action. This effigy is a demonstration of faithfulness and gratitude,

endowed by the last descendants of the *Tibon* family to pay tribute to their ancestor, and also to remind us that it was here, at the entrance to the *Realejo* district, that the long-forgotten Jewish quarter, *Garnata Alhayad*, occupied the hill known as *La Sabica*, which lay beneath the walls of the Arab fortress and stretched from the *Torres Bermejas* to the *Campo del Príncipe*, near to which they erected their synagogue, on the site where the church of *San Cecilio* stands today. Not a single trace remains of that quarter. Following the occupation of Granada by the forces of Castille and the edict signed in that same city on the 31 March 1942 ordering the expulsion of the Jews ("... we agree to order the said Jews and Jewesses to leave our kingdoms and never to return to any one of them"), the Jewish quarter was utterly demolished and the grounds sequestered for the conquerors' palaces, convents and towers, the buildings with which the city is nowadays identified. This modern statue cannot rectify that past act of fanaticism but it does open up a crack in the darkness of oblivion, making it less unanimous, less final.

Scarcely anybody looks at statues nowadays, no one understands them. We've got used to them, just as we have the trees and lamp-posts. It is as though they did not exist. Their value can, however, only be upheld if they are looked at by passers-by.

Some of the last of Granada's bootblacks work in a corner of *plaza Mariana Pineda*, which the locals call familiarly "*Marian's Square*". The bootblack who used to clean my grandfather's shoes was paralytic and on rainy days would sell lottery tickets in the shelter of the arcade in *calle Ganivet*, sitting on a little red trolley. From him I learnt among other things that there is more than one use that playing-cards can be put to. I remember how he would extract a couple of grubby, cracked cards from the box he kept his brushes and polish in, which also had a little rest on the lid for the client to put his foot on, and insert them between my grandfather's shoes and socks so as not to stain the socks while applying the polish. I remember the dexterity with which he slapped the brush from one hand to the other, the dignity with which he carried out such a humble task, and above all something he said to me one day. "Look boy," he said, pointing at a statue in the middle of the square, "that's the only woman up on a pedestal who's neither a queen nor a virgin.". I don't suppose I replied, as I didn't understand what he meant until many years later, when someone told me the story of the young widow who in 1831 was sent to her death at the garrote, accused of sheltering a fugitive of the law, a liberal conspirator, for whom she had embroidered —for love some say— a banner flourishing one word: LIBERTAD. Some of the old folks still recall the words to romantic elegies lamenting her execution. In 1837 the people began to honour her name with a popular festival, and her ashes were turned into an object of worship and paraded around the city as though they were a venerable relic. It was an extravagant tribute to a victim of political intolerance, the only local holiday which ignored the dictates of the religious calendar. After the civil war it was prohibited but since the return to democracy it has been reinstated, or rather, reinvented, and a civic procession, a simple parade of members of the local authorities, makes its way without any ceremonial fuss or pomp from *plaza de Mariana Pineda* to what was a piece of waste-ground, now *plaza de la Libertad*, and the destination of all public protest marches. Here a monolith stands to mark the spot where she was executed and for a couple of days in May this stone serves as a focal point for festivities and a somewhat devitalized remembrance. Now I understand that the bootblack, who, I found out some years later, was a communist and had suffered a long history of illness, had been expressing his gratitude and admiration, and *Mariana Pineda* remains for me the only woman raised on a pedestal who is neither queen nor virgin.

Statues are now an outdated way of paying homage. The local authorities no longer undertake this commitment. It is difficult to imagine them erecting a monument today such as the one dedicated to *Angel Ganivet* in the poplar groves of the

Alhambra, or the one that the Arts Centre erected in the gardens on the banks of the *River Genil* to the memory of *Julio Quesada Cañavera y Piédrola*, who, among his many ranks of nobility, held the title of *Duke of San Pedro de Galatino*. He became a sugar magnate, pioneered the building of the *Alhambra Palace Hotel* —that epitome of fakery which now forms so much a part of Granada's skyline— and encouraged the construction of the road to the Sierra Nevada, on whose flanks he built the *Hotel del Duque*. We knew nothing about any of this in the days when we wound up to the valley of *San Juan* in the tram-car, which has since been dismantled in the name of progress, and is now the kind of journey that you can make only in civilized, northern countries. Nowadays we either pay no tribute at all or resort to a bust or an abstract monument, which signifies either everything or nothing at all. One associates statues, not without some measure of disdain, with speeches and pigeons, French-style gardens and Scandinavian neatness, blond children, nannies in bonnets being pestered by infantrymen, of nineteenth-century novels and English films, a story-book image of a yesteryear we never had. They seem ridiculous and out of place, abandoned in the middle of squares where no one goes to sit, like the statue of *Alonso Cano*, the humanist painter and sculpture, which now stands alongside the cathedral façade which he designed. Or that of *Fray Luis de*

Granada, indefatigable preacher of the Catholic faith, which can be seen today in *plaza de Santo Domingo*, adjacent to the convent of *Santa Cruz la Real*, where he taught. Or the statue erected in *plaza de la Universidad* in honour of the *Emperor Charles V*, who founded the University of Granada in 1526 with the aim of producing, "...excellent theologians and stalwart preachers of the Christian faith". The fate of this particular statue is nowadays to be dressed up in outlandish attire on the patron saint's day of the students of the *Law Faculty* on the other side of the square, and to be draped with plastic buckets and swathed with scraps of cloth and remain like that sometimes for months on end until the wind and the rain rid him of his comic garb. These figures hidden away in parks or lost in the solitude of squares are the expression of a civic pride that was wont to praise effort, initiative and sacrifice, to recognise the nobler side of the common people's history. Statues give material form to the relationship the city establishes with the artificers of its past, with the men and women who have contributed to making Granada what it is. They prevent us from forgetting that the city is a collective effort, that things which now form part of our everyday lives once did not exist, that they have been conceived and carried out with will and determination. Bronze and marble redeem some of these men from oblivion and grant them the privilege of being remembered.

There is some mysterious message from the past in statues. In *plaza del Padre Suárez* —which is not actually a square but a small piece of waste-ground jammed with parked cars opposite the birthplace of *Francisco Suárez*—, who was "a distinguished commentator upon Aristotle and St. Thomas, an enlightened philosopher, profound theologian, outstanding legal expert and such an eloquent defender of the Catholic church that he was worthy to be named by the Holy See *Doctor Eximio*, glory to the church, illustrious member of the Company of Jesus, honour to Spain, and one of the most distinguished Sons of this City", according to the plaque fastened to its wall —there stands a monument to the memory of *Isidoro Maiquez*, an actor who was born in Cartagena and died in Granada in 1820. It was erected by the town council of the day as a token of gratitude for his contribution to the city. The monument remains but we know next to nothing about those times or the people who lived then. A stone column is all that remains of an important gesture made in the past which nobody understands any more. In a hundred years' time when this frantic age filled with so many events has faded into oblivion, more than one citizen will stand before the statue of *Agustín Lara* and wonder what strange motives inspired a Mexican to put up a statue in honour of a fellow countryman who devoted his time to writing songs.

As important as it is to recognise the work of our predecessors in the construction of our city, Granada is also the sum of many more humble efforts, inventions and customs which often go unnoticed. In some Swedish cities there are sculptures scattered all over the parks and streets which, instead of paying tribute to genius or to outstanding works, honour the unknown heroes of everyday life: a florist, a musician, a builder, a pedlar, a pensioner. They are not raised on pedestals, standing in stately mien looking down on the people, but are represented in ordinary postures, leaning against a lamp-post, sitting on a park bench, standing on the pavement waiting for a bus. It is a way of remembering the nameless men and women who have no great attributes other than their citizenship and their work, but without whom towns would be little more than vast stone wildernesses.

There is a tendency to judge a city by its strange and eccentric characters: in Granada the lanky old fellow, who wanders around the streets in a short skirt like a ballerina's, his white hair gathered into a bun on top of his head, always alone, always in a hurry, always carrying an empty basket, indifferent to the jeering or pitying looks that follow him; or the fat, dumb girl, with a permanent grin stamped on her round pudding face, gripping a grey box to collect coins in, whose wonderful and perverse joy it is to stand beside someone who has stopped to look in a shop window and suddenly nudge the unsuspeching citizen as hard as she can with her hip, chuckling at her mischievous prank and the ridiculous shocked expression on the victim's face; the lame beggar on his knees with his arms flung straight out sideways forming a cross of his whole body; his crutches lie on the pavement, he dresses in the purple shirt of a penitent with a yellow cord tied round his neck, requesting and expressing his gratitude for offerings in a loud, ringing voice like that of a priest and with a dignified composure, all of which would be difficult to understand were it not for the fact that he has converted the business of public charity into a serious office; old women who wander erratically around the city dragging behind them piles of cardboard boxes tied together with string; emaciated, ghost-like priests in their cassocks and shovel hats; an idiot who strides around the streets dressed in short, baggy trousers, scruffy old sandals, and a sweater over his shoulders, buttoned only at the neck, making it look like a prince's cape in a fairy tale; a one-armed musician beseeching the charity of passers by with his left hand while performing an out-of-tune version of Andalucía's anthem on a harmonica held in his right. Despite this however, it is those men who have nothing outstanding about them, who go to the office, the market, the bank, the hospital, the football stadium, the cemetery, and the cinema, who do the same thing at the same time, every day for years on end, who best characterize a city. The buildings, streets and shops can all be copied and reproduced elsewhere but no man is the same as another; his identity is unique. Cities are a made up of swarms of harmless men and women, indistinguishable one from another in most ways, unnoticed by anybody, who are nevertheless as singular as the ones everybody points at. It is the inhabitants who make one city distinct from another, their habits, their obsessions, their daily routines, which are impossible to copy perfectly anywhere else. Granada is a unique combination of almost identical events repeated unconsciously by certain people at the same time every day. The city evolves with each tiny action of its inhabitants: the buying of somewhere to live, the death of an old woman, the beginning of a friendship, the signing of a business agreement, two teenagers meeting each other for the first time, the arrival of a villager; all insignificant incidents which will never be chronicled nor commemorated by statues or engraved on tablets, but which bring about changes in the city, making it more open and less backward.

Posters are like the leaves of a calendar, but one which is not ruled by the movement of the stars, only by chance and the whim of men. Their survival or demise on the wall is determined by the rain, the wind or by other posters stuck on top of them so that sometimes they are hidden from view even before they have fulfilled the mission they were intended for. Posters mark the invisible, arbitrary rhythm of the city. They broadcast news, they advertise, they tell us about an ephemeral, evanescent Granada, which is destined to sink into oblivion; they announce the arrival of a circus, the departure times for a trip, the presentation of a new book, an anti-war march, an appeal for our vote, the production of a new stain remover. Stuck on the walls of the steep and winding *calle Calderería* are posters vilifying the commemoration of January 2, when Moorish Granada capitulated to the *Catholic Monarchs*. It is an old, routine ritual which the years have deprived of any passion or pride it may once have had. The posters give voice to the dissenting, offended calls of men and women who claim to be the descendants of these same Moors, converted to Islam, which has modified the course of their lives, their names and the way they dress. Once, in the face of a young woman, half-covered in a light-blue shawl, who could often be seen going up and down *calle Calderería,* I thought I recognised a girl whom I had seen at another time serving drinks in a fashionable pub. The presence of these young neophytes, their tiny shops, the strange alphabet of some of their signs, reinforce the image we get of a simulated Moslem enclave, an attempt to reinstate a world which occupied that space for centuries, but which is now surrounded by other streets, other customs, other ways of life. From the top window of a house in the *Albaicín*, which makes shift as a mosque, five times a day you can hear the wailing of the muezzin —an erstwhile left-wing militant it is rumoured— calling the new Moslems to prayer, deserters from other doctrines who have found in the restoration of the past a form of self-justification, a cause. The new followers of Islam are trying to reconstruct, with a fervour which brooks no despair, a way of life that history had once confined to the farther shores of the Mediterranean. In their illusory return to the city of the past they are looking for a refuge from the tribulations of the present.

A city always grows as the reflection of another which preceded it and which it tries to imitate. When the Syrians landed on primitive Iliberis, bringing whit them in their minds the image of Damascus, this land reminded them of their homeland and they tried to make a copy of it here. The Arabs who later visited Granada described it as being a replica of Damascus. The palm trees and myrtle bushes, the irrigation channels and the cunningly designed buildings were all made in the image of the capital city of Syria which they kept alive in their memories. Centuries later the adventurers who migrated to America tried to reproduce

Granada in the lands they conquered, and thus other Granadas, similar to the last redoubt of the Arabs in Spain, sprang up on the other side of the ocean. Perhaps cities are nothing more than imperfect imitations of one vast original city that no longer exists. Some are replicas inspired by pride; others, like those built by the Arabs after they fled from Granada, are built upon nostalgia. When they abandoned Granada the exiles fixed a last image of the city in their minds so that they could make an imitation in the lands that were waiting for them on the other side of the sea. It was a way of comforting their sorrows at having to relinquish Granada. And although the cities which later rose up did not perfectly mirror the one they had left behind everyone accepted the pretence, the illusion that they were still living in the city which had been so unjustly wrested from them. Each new generation has inherited —along with their family names, heirlooms and an ever dimmer memory of the past— the desire to return to the primordial city, of which the cities where they have lived —Fez, Tetuan, Tangier and Temden— are but imperfect, provisional copies.

Five hundred years later young North Africans, men from the same cities which welcomed the exiles from Granada, go down to the beach on nights when the sea is calm and the moon full and in the anonymity of darkness board small, fragile rowing boats. Their goal is the northern shore, so close yet seemingly so fortified against them. Their purpose is not to return to the promised land nor to reconquer the lands of their ancestors, but to beg for a job, to find the honourable future they believe they deserve. Huddled together, shaking with fear and damp, against which their only protection is a woollen cap, an old jersey and a short-sleeved jacket, they abandon their homeland without regret and without a backward glance. They disappear into the gloomy uncertainty of the Mediterranean, silent and motionless, cowering beneath a blanket, resisting the desire to smoke in case the glow should give them away, watchful for the tenuous lights of the closing coast, alert to the sound of strange voices and foreign accents, spurred on by the hope of a new life, one which could not be more humiliating than the miserable future they are leaving behind. If the sea does not swallow them up they will disembark in some small cove, and swim the last few metres with the same terror one experiences when trying to escape from a nightmare, as though their lives depended on that frantic whirling of arms. Then, as stealthily as they crossed the sea, they disperse and head for prearranged addresses. I have seen them some time later in the streets of Granada selling piles of heavy rugs, which hang over their arms like bats' wings, or working on building sites or as casual labourers on the land, a land that was first tilled by men with the same names as theirs. They are always pointed at and treated unjustly, feared by their neighbours, who regard their dark skin, ebony eyes, curly hair, sharp noses, timid smiles, and foreign tongue with deep mistrust. Granada for them is the city which holds their future. The past, if they are lucky, will remain on the other shore. Granada is a land inhabited at one and the same time by nostalgia and hopes for the future.

Still to be seen on the corner of a house which has survived with more courage than splendour is a plaque bearing the name *calle del Ciego o Arjona*, which no longer exists and cannot now be found in any street guide, but which in the not-too-distant past was written on the envelopes of letters coming from other provinces, below Christian names and surnames that identified men and women who day after day for years on end were witness in this phantasmagorical place to such constant and undeniable processes as death and dawn. In days gone by this wide stretch of waste-ground, occasionally used as a car park, was a residential quarter and had a name, *San Lázaro*; it had streets and houses with numbers over their doors, people living there who with their tales and anecdotes gave it life and registered it in our memories. Now it is a vast, empty space overrun with rats and regarded with indifference or disgust by the passers-by. But part of Granada also survives in this waste-ground, a city as real as that which we can see around us today. Granada is just as much the name of an invisible city, whose reality we take for granted as unquestionably as we accept the existence of ancestors we never knew, who have handed down to us their names and also their defects, maybe also a nickname, who bore those who in turn gave birth to us, and who were the origin of those faces we have known, our grandparents and parents whom we take after and love without needing to question why. Empty spaces are the absent faces of cities that once existed, more numerous than the Granada of today, which is only one of the faces of the city that has been calling itself Granada for over two thousand years. If everything that has been lost during that time could be reconstructed Granada would be another city, very different from the one we know today, which shares few common elements with the previous ones. A city is the sum of all its empty spaces. The city we have been calling Granada for the last few centuries is not the same one as that seen by so many other eyes throughout the ages. The difference is not marked either by the subjectivity of the viewer or by the size of the city, but in what is missing. It differs not in what one can see but in the things one can no longer see. The shape of a city owes as much to destruction as to creation.

The struggle between what it once was and what it is, between what we see and what we remember, governs the way in which the people who live there see their city. The buildings in the *Gran Vía de Colón*, which today constitute such an indelible image of the city, replaced others which in their day also seemed equally unchangeable. The history of a city is also the history of its demolished buildings. Granada is the name of a ghostly city, a city of open spaces, vanished houses and the bones of erstwhile palaces.

Destruction has many faces. To a great extent a city is the work of fire. It would be useless to try to list all the buildings destroyed by fire since the city was founded: convents, markets, palaces and houses. The face of Granada has been fashioned by the accidental spark and the deliberate, purifying flame. The streets of Granada have also seen days of uprising and revolt, bands of revolutionaries intent on using the torch to cure the ills of the past. An ephemeral and misguided army, they set fire to churches, theatres and fashionable clubs in the belief that they were removing the obstacles to social progress, without realising —and this lesson is slow and painful to learn, the final wisdom to come from defeat— that ideas outlive ashes with consummate ease.

Vista de Sierra Navada desde el Collado de la Gitana.

Vista de la Laguna de Río Seco

◊ Doble página anterior: Vista del Albaicín desde la Torre de la Vela.
◊◊◊ 6 páginas precedentes: vista desde la Catedral.

Plaza de San Nicolás.

Doble página siguiente: Fuente del Tomate en otoño. ◊ **3 dobles páginas siguientes: vista desde la Alcazaba.** ◊◊◊

◁◁ **Torre de las Damas.** ◁ **Partal.**

Our Granada of today has grown on top of the rubble produced by the religious fanaticism of the Castillian conquerors. Almost all the churches and convents that we can see in the old quarter of the *Albaicín* were built on the remains of old mosques, the only clue to the previous existence of which lies in the abandoned remains of nearby water cisterns for the faithful to purify themselves before worship. The new religious edifices were erected as a demonstration of authority, to aid the education and conversion of the converted Moors who stayed on in the city, and to chastise the memory of the defeated Moslems by establishing symbols of the new religion where their places of worship had been. Centuries later a new fanaticism expelled the nuns and monks and emptied the convents, which were then demolished or occupied by soldiers and state bureaucrats. Public squares were cleared from the rubble of cloisters, *plaza del Carmen, plaza de la Trinidad, plaza de San Agustín,* all of which are today inseparable features of the city.

Progress and modernity were also the pretext for a savage destruction of the city. It was during a time, still not completely passed, when everything old was considered to be decadent, an intolerable blemish on a modern city. The past was considered quite simply to be a shameful inheritance. Advances in technology and the sciences were interpreted as heralding an age of prosperity and eternal well being. Anything old, features that once had given the city its note of distinction, got in the way of the brave new Granada and were now merely shabby and obtrusive. Throughout the last two centuries city walls, churches, palaces, and indeed whole districts have been knocked down with such fervour that the list of buildings demolished is greater than a complete catalogue of those still standing. In 1923 *Leopoldo Torres Balbás* declared that with all the buildings pulled down since the beginning of the nineteenth century up to that year a new city could be built. Seventy years later we have enough rubble to construct yet another one.

The tenacity with which the speculators have destroyed Granada is an object lesson in determination. There was a time indeed when so frenzied was the annihilation rate of all that was old that one walked through the streets wondering whether what one could see that afternoon would still be standing the following morning. During the antisocial days of *Franco's* dictatorship, instead of rejoicing in the gift of a marvellous city we used to celebrate every morning the miracle of its survival, the good fortune to have something left to admire despite the supreme valour of the devastators. Granada is the product of a swashbuckling love of destruction which began with the first mosque demolished after the Christian conquest and has continued without abatement until our own times, during which a town councillor recently justified the digging of an underground car-park on the site of a Moorish cemetery by claiming that the cars of the quick were worth far more than the miserable bones of the dead. It should come as no surprise that in a city which praises itself for the excellence of its remote antiquity and condones the flattening of anything not deemed to conform with these principles, the memory of what has been lost is stronger than the esteem in which what actually exists is held

Granada is at one and the same time what is and what has been. A moment arrives in the lives of all city dwellers when the sum of what they have known in the past is more than what remains for them to see in the future. For them the Granada that once was is more real than the city they live in and the history of their lives is more an inventory of ruins than a catalogue of things existing. Their eyes, accustomed to seeing street lamps, corners and pebbled paths that once existed, register what is no longer there rather than what is before them. They walk along streets that they alone can see, through a city lying beneath and behind the present one. We don't all walk along the same streets although they may have had the same name for years on end: some people, when they go down the *Avenida de la Constitución* are passing along a wide avenue full of traffic lights and lined with tall modern buildings and glass-plated offices, while others continue to stroll down a quiet boulevard in the shade of lime and acacia trees, where during the summer tables and chairs are set out haphazardly in the street in front of bars, all of which one fine day was suddenly and shamefully swept away and covered with asphalt. Streets remembered from childhood, with iron balconies and their ground floors given over to an ice-making factory or a chemist's shop, which also sold sandpaper and turpentine, bear the same names as the streets of today, with hotels, banks, doorways with metal plaques announcing the names of doctors, lawyers and advertising agencies. Granada is the name of a city erected upon waste lots and the memories of those who walk every day along its modern streets.

No one ever explained those narrow alleys to me. We learned surreptitiously, awkwardly, exchanging secret suspicions, which were confirmed gradually as the soft, embarrassing down grew on our faces in confirmation of our virility. They were at first mysterious warrens in the depths of which shadows flitted furtively, half-lit by the dimmest of bulbs. We didn't venture into them, without really knowing why but fearing some nameless punishment. Then, in answer to the manhood burgeoning within us, we dared to stroll leisurely along the pavement past their entrances, putting on a false air of assurance, trying to look towards them with unconcern, with a challenge in our eyes even. We measured our manliness in what we deemed to be roguery and defiance. And the day inevitably arrived when pride obliged us to stop showing off and put an end to this self-imposed restraint against entering that forbidden realm. And we were indeed amazed by what we found there; it hadn't occurred to any of us that the bodies of these women could be so shapeless, so like someone's mother's, so different from the bodies we glimpsed under the clothes of the girls we silently adored. The garbage, the familiar mewing of cats, the doorways lit with a single bulb, the obscene sniggers of the soldiers, the heavily made-up faces of those women, who we hardly dared glance toward, some with their hair in rollers, scarcely covered up in quilted house-coats identical to those that housewives wear when they take the rubbish out to the dustbin in the evenings, all joined to finally abolish a myth and nudge us that bit further past adolescence.

When I look at the whores nowadays, stationed in the sun at the corner of *calle Jazmín*, trying to get away from the damp and squalor of those alleyways, in wait for a client more in need of talk than sex, I never fail to remember my dim-wittedness, my narrow fantasies of youth, my uncalled-for sixteen years. But looking at them today, with neither lust nor fear, surrounded by scaffolding, builders in hard hats and blue overalls singing snatches of song, surveyors making notes on plans, with the rebuilding of the *San Matías* quarter at hand and their extinction inevitable, I see in them the last vestiges of a crumbling past, of customs which until now have survived the erosion of time, more resistant than the metals and marbles that the buildings themselves are made of. They are what remains of the ancient brothels of the *Manigua* district, which from the sixteenth century onwards flourished around *plaza Campillo*, in the shadow of the stretch of city wall that ran between the *Bibataubín* and *Bibarrambla* gates. Since that time houses have tumbled down around *San Matías*, the city has been transformed several times over, palaces and theatres have been demolished, streets and squares have been opened up, completely changing the face of the city, but until today the brothels have resisted, gradually shrinking inwards, closed in by decay and ruin.

When in those days we loitered along those pavements with just enough cockiness to cover up our cowardice we still believed that with every step we were treading a fresh path, that our passing was prophetic. We needed to believe ourselves the first and only ones. We were young and ignorant. We could never imagine that the same path which to us was unexplored had been trodden by feet much older than ours. We were not to know then that the city is an accumulation of routes, of rituals, of quests repeated generation after generation, time and again, almost unconsciously. Granada is a web of tracks that one follows mistakenly believing oneself to be the master of one's direction. But every city imposes its own particular ways upon us, puts us on paths leading to places that others have discovered before us, paths where nevertheless we leave our own light footprint. The city is the sum of certain routines, customs and gestures whose origins we never need enquire into. After their defeat the Moors who stayed on in Spain were made to bury their language, change their way of dress, abandon their ceremonies; their food, music and religious observances were all corrupted to disguise their origins; their books were burnt and even their names altered; they had to change everything including the very way they walked and talked so that all links with the past should be completely severed. But neither threats nor decrees nor harassment, nor the tortures inflicted upon them by the Inquisition could entirely obliterate the depths of their memories. Five centuries later, after violent attempts to uproot the culture of the defeated Arabs, scattered traces still survive. Their legacy lives on in the fingers of the potters in the *Albaicín*, who repeat the very same movements that their forebears made to coax out the *Fajalauza* ceramic ware; it survives in the courses of the irrigation channels carrying water to gardens and cisterns, in the way of laying bricks just so to build a vault, in the baking of loaves in domed, wood-fired ovens, in a certain tendency towards secrecy and indolence. They are all traditions as irrefutable as names themselves. Words bear witness to the passing of these Moorish folk through these lands: "albañil, gandul, cifra, ajuar, zaguán, jarabe, almocafre, maroma, jazmín, zahorí, acequia…"* and their blood, an infinitesimal part of their now impure blood, still irremediably moulds the features of the people of this city. The past resides in gestures, habits, tastes, in simple things we have inherited without ever having thought about it, and which we pass on to others with equally unconscious faithfulness. We feel change as something that despoils and mutilates the past irreparably. Change always seems to arrive on

----

* builder, good-for-nothing, number, trousseau, hall, syrup, hoe, rope, jasmine, dowser, irrigation channel.

the arm of vengeance, the imposition of the victor, intruders from other lands, strangers to the original city. One can only sympathize with the anger and impatience of the vanquished and their determination to guard the frontiers of their memory even when it is not one's own.

In *Zacatín*, a street which, true to the meaning of its name in Arabic, "street of the second-hand-clothes sellers", remains a street of small shops, there is one tiny shop in particular tucked into the middle of a row of more luxurious establishments that sells hats, caps and berets and which seems to come from a novel by *Benito Pérez Galdos*. It has been there for time immemorial, as though it had forgotten to die. And there it stays, alone, disregarded, without offspring, eternally on the point of death. In the window hats and caps of all kinds are lined up like trophies, scrupulously marked with prices as anachronous as the goods themselves. Nothing you can think of wearing on your head is missing from that shop window: woollen balaclavas, deerstalkers, panama hats...; it is the same today as when I first looked into it. That first time I gazed with surprise, now I regard it with admiration, in praise of the determination of the place, the indomitable courage and skill which has enabled it to survive unchanged for so long. Around and about I have seen businesses come and go with the same inevitable rhythm that has gone into my growing up, their display windows changing in tune with the tastes of the times, their frontages becoming adorned with marble and their goods protected with alarms and armour-plated doors. But the green and grey door of this lone shop has stayed the same, as though condemned to await an unlikely revival in the popularity of the trilby and the cloth cap.

One spends half one's life looking into shop windows. There are shops, just as there are bars and cinemas, which form such an inextricable part of our lives that only when they close down or we move away do they acquire a meaning for us that we hardly suspected during the days when we were regular customers. We could construct a history of our lives around the windows of the shops we have remained loyal to, those which held the things we desired: the toys, the cakes and pastries, and the fountain pens and loose-leaf files, and the trousers with that prestigious name tag, and the books. Shop windows define a city and define us as well. That hat shop belongs to a lineage of shops which have always dispensed personal service across the counter, selling things that now seem to belong to a Granada of another age: fine lace, buttons of inconceivable shapes and colours, woven hemp baskets, mats, saddles, esparto ropes and plaited thongs, and the spices and gut to make sausages when the pigs are slaughtered. They are secret bazaars hidden in among rows of modern temples paying homage to the beauty of wrinkles, exclusively designed jewellery and audiovisual high technology. They are relics of another world rather than another time, the remains of a city traversed in due season by flocks of sheep and goats following the lines of ancient tracks that have been cut off abruptly by asphalt streets, and pavements running parallel to water channels as old as the city itself, which overflow onto the path on irrigation days; a city where strings of donkeys lived in peace with petrol-engined motor cars, where office workers rubbed shoulders with farm workers crossing the city in the evenings, scythe over one shoulder, their mules laden with baskets of tomatoes and artichokes and a bundle of furze for the animals, on their way home to where a pig was kept in the pen for slaughter come the cold of winter. In those days the customers went to cafés to while away the hours after lunch or to close a deal on the sale of livestock, and children went to buy milk from the local cowherd. The knife grinder announced his arrival by whistling on a set of Pan's pipes as he peddled his bike with its little circular grindstone on the back, the chair mender worked in the street reseating rush-bottomed chairs and the tinker repaired holes in worn-out pots and pans. Even now on sunny days just such a chair mender, indifferent to the bustle and the rushing feet of passers by, the surprised glances of children on their way to school, squats down in a doorway in the *Avenida de la Constitución*. It's his trade, he says, and there's no way he's going to give it up.

He is a last vestige of a Granada where long, black, hired cars used to arrive every day from Guadix and Baza, from the Alpujarra mountains, from Alhama, and even from the outlying areas of surrounding provinces, to park around *plaza de la Trinidad*. The passengers would get out slowly and silently, dressed in their Sunday best, men in corduroy suits, tieless with the top button of their white shirts done up, woman in black wearing woollen cardigans and a medallion of their village's patron saint around their necks. From there they would spread out through the city to the ironmongers' and the workshops of the esparto weavers, to carry out the errands they had carefully noted down, to arrive punctually at the optician's or the rheumatologist's, to renew their national identity cards and wearily follow a tortuous procession of shop counters, offices, stores, sales windows and doctors' surgeries with X-ray machines. Finally they would have lunch at the inns surrounding the square before returning in the afternoon to their villages in the same cars that brought them, bursting now at the seams.

Maybe the Granada of my imagination wasn't really like that and I am unwittingly confusing memories with inventions of my own collected from phrases heard at random, images created by men in suede windcheaters with woollen collars sitting in some gentlemen's club, the clip-clopping of mule hoofs in the streets of my childhood, oddments I have read, snatches of conversation overheard from the old folks sitting in *plaza de la Pescadería*. And those old shop windows, surviving like villages swallowed up by the greedy water of a reservoir, whose names only live on in the memories of their last inhabitants or on old maps and road signs that the Ministry of Public Works has forgotten to take down, villages that emerge suddenly in years of drought, revealing church towers, weather cocks and chimneys, sometimes even walls on which the shield of a noble family can still be made out, the skeleton of a village laboriously built up and lived in for generations. These somewhat eccentric shops form part of a town that we no longer perceive, a world that has been relentlessly dismantled, close to us but just out of our reach, a world that only survives in these shop windows, which unashamedly bear witness

to the old rural face of Granada that has long since been banished from the city.

From around midday onwards a group of young vagrants gather in a corner of *plaza Alonso Cano* accompanied by a harmless scraggy mongrel. They are young men and women who don't seem to be particularly ill-treated by life, although their rags and matted hair try to belie the impression. They carry patched-up rucksacks and musical instruments, a recorder, a guitar, a tambourine, which they improvise on in the hope of scrounging a couple of bob from the passers-by in this pedestrian precinct. For those who remember *Bob Dylan* these wayfarers, albeit a bit scruffier, must remind them of the Woodstock festival or protesters against the Vietnam war on American university campuses. Litre bottles of beer have replaced wine in the ancient ritual of drinking silently together without swapping a word. They sit on the ground in the shelter of the wall of the *Cura Eclasiástica*, which, according to the twisted metal sign stuck to it, was from its foundation until the middle of the eighteenth century the seat of the *University of Granada*. The mongrel regards them sombrely, as though staying with them were its profession, bored and indifferent like a bodyguard. This square and the adjoining *plaza de las Pasiegas* are places of transit. The well-washed citizens with their looks of disdain don't seem to realise that these casual gatherings of vagabonds are the only events that give some sort of life from time to time to these inhospitable and empty squares. The people who rush across, urged on by who knows what unpostponable business are offended by idleness, a life that isn't ordered by the clock, the silent, wounding reproach of the vagrants, who take life so nonchalantly and measure time with neither blame nor anxiety. They know that they will leave no trace behind them in their passing through the city, and they don't care.

An austere cathedral dominates the square just some few feet in front of them. The construction of its walls and arches marks two centuries in the history of the city. The building of a cathedral constitutes a victory over the remorseless march of time. In 1704, when it was agreed that the work was finished —more through exhaustion of the will to go on than because the project was complete— almost two hundred years had elapsed since its original plan had been drawn up in 1505, just after the first uprisings in Granada of the *Moriscos*, the Moors who had agreed to be baptized and stayed on after the Christian conquest. Throughout these two centuries kings and dynasties came and went in Spain, and in Granada itself uncountable mayors, military governors and archbishops ruled and died leaving little or no trace of their passing. When the first stone was laid in 1523 the city had been scourged by two bouts of plague coming up from the port of Málaga. Colonization of the distant, boundless Americas had begun. Every day galleys were tying up in new-world ports laden with half-starved fortune hunters, greedy, visionary soldiers with sword in hand, friars armed with a cross, a syllabary and a grammar in their scrips, farmers loaded with sacks of new seeds, noblemen eager for glory and whores with an eye for an easy fortune. *Hernán Cortés* had begun the bloody conquest of Mexico, torturing *Cuauhtemoc*, emperor of the Aztecs, with a cruelty only matched some years later by *Francisco Pizarro* when he executed the Inca *Atahualpa*. Motivated by fantastic expectation and ambition the emigrants disembarked hoping to find *Eldorado*, the worldly Eden they had dreamed of, the prodigal land where fortune was the rightful gift of nature rather than the laborious fruit of years of toil. The colonizers tilled barren plains, explored mountains and jungles from California to Tierra del Fuego, lands hitherto unseen by European eyes, enslaved the natives, robbed them of their idols and myths and spread the gospel in strange tongues; two Basque sailors, *Fernando de Magallanes* and *Juan Sebastián Elcano*, circumnavigated the earth, determining for the first time its shape and size, and while all this was happening stone masons and builders in Granada were cutting trenches laying the foundations for pillars, erecting scaffolding, and the work on the cathedral —often held up because of plague, disagreements within the town council and the death or dismissal of successions of architects— went slowly ahead. Over the years, as labourers rigged pulleys and mixed mortar, as keystones were dropped into arches and the finishing touches were put to chapels, the *Council of Trent* was convened and the *Inquisition* pursued heretics and sectarians, the *Moriscos* were repressed with the same fury that they had unleashed in their uprising and sporadic rebellions broke out over the price of bread. At the same time, over the space of twenty years, one of the most enormous palaces in the western world, the *Escorial*, was completed as both court and monastic retreat for *King Philip II*, Spanish troops triumphed throughout Europe, alliances were made and broken at whim from one day to the next, countries were annexed and cities sacked, tremendous battles were fought both at sea and across the fallow fields of a whole continent. The world changed and grew in rhythm with the works on the cathedral. Nothing was delayed in its just course, neither birth nor death, neither ruin nor artistic creation. In *Juan de la Cueva's* printing house in Madrid the first edition of a novel was brought out by an old soldier and tax collector, *Miguel de Cervantes*, entitled, "*Don Quixote de la Mancha*", Diego Velázquez painted in his studio, the comedies of *Lope de Vega* were being put on for the first time in courtyards and theatres and the religious plays of *Calderón de la Barca* were presented at religious festivals to mark *Corpus Christi; Soto de Rojas* in his house in the *Albaicín* wrote the verses to "*Jardín abierto para pocos, paraíso cerrado para muchos*" in the style of *Luis de Góngora*, and the cathedral continued to grow. Masons hewed stone from Sierra Elvira, vaults were arched over and the transept roofed in.

When work on the cathedral, originally conceived as a replica of the *Church of the Holy Sepulchre*, was deemed to be complete, the world was not the same: frontiers had moved, tastes and fashions were different, new inventions had changed the way men went about their work; the very faces of cities had altered. But little has come down to us of what lay behind all this effort, of so many generations who formed the backbone of the city. Two centuries of city life petrified in one immense block of stone. A city is a weft of disparate times and Granada is the fruition of many individual labours. The mark of some has been only ephemeral, as tenuous as a footprint in the sand on a beach, whilst the work of others will remain as indelible as those left by the astronauts in the dust on the moon, never to be obliterated by wind or rain.

Every once in a while the bus companies or the town council fiddle around with bus stops; they take away shelters, change cement for plastic, install seats, put up boards for advertisements and paint the shelters a different colour. They also change the buses themselves; they make them more spacious, the seats more comfortable, pleasanter to ride in, with piped music and air conditioning. The buses and the stops change but the passengers stay the same: the same look and way of standing as they wait, the same air of resignation handed down from father to son. Archetype city dwellers can always be found waiting in groups at bus stops. Early in the morning almost no one is waiting at the stop, it serves as a reception point for people arriving from out of town. The buses pull up with a strident screech of brakes and the passengers get off with fixed determination, to disappear hastily into the surrounding streets. They come from outlying suburbs, the names of which can be read at the front of the bus. The regularity with which this loading and unloading operation takes place is proportionally inverse to the hour of the day. At the end of the morning the same passengers who got off some hours before await once more the arrival of their bus, probably the same one which brought them there. They form a static, amorphous mass, which only breaks up on sight of the bus. If the bus is held up by an unexpected traffic jam they get impatient and shake their heads in annoyance; they murmur and look from their watches to the horizon and back again with a mixture of desperation and disgust. Some flick through the newspaper. From time to time another might open a book, lean against the posters on the wall and with admirable detachment lose himself in his reading. Pensioners are the most orderly; they know their timetables and the exact spot the bus pulls up at, and so they take up positions where they can scramble on first and grab a seat, bus-passes at the ready. The buses turn up unannounced and stop with an almost human sigh of air and the mass condenses around the doors. Some minutes later they are off to another city, also called Granada, which has grown up around the town that strangers identify as the true Granada. A newish city this, but born with the same decrepitude that marks all things precarious. It grew up to accommodate a gradual inundation of pilgrims who arrived in flight from the poverty of the land, attracted by the siren song of the city, the call of the cement mixers and the cranes, the sound of the development and welfare they had never enjoyed. For them this new prosperity was enshrined in a job on a building site or cleaning the stairs in a block of flats, in eventually being able to buy their own apartment in a building with a lift, and then a washing machine, a television and maybe their own car one day. The blocks of flats are only distinguishable by the numbers on the wall outside, lumps of red brick which the eye never stays to dwell on, façades with washing hanging from barred windows and dripping into streets with the same look as streets the world over, streets duplicated in a thousand towns, with the same empty cement-ringed beds for trees that will never be planted, streets that run out into immense waste-grounds covered in rubble and hoardings where posters advertise modern televisions and tremendous bargains at the big stores, empty lots where children and mules live together among the remains of rusty, scrapped cars. Their exodus meant a tremendous wrench: they abandoned the places where their ancestors were buried, left behind their customs, their way of life, their beliefs and the stories that made sense to them of the events taking place in the world. Nothing in that peripheral Granada is worth photographing, except perhaps to illustrate a catalogue of ugliness, but nevertheless its inhabitants, whose memories are rooted in distant parts, give life to the old, inner city, the Granada exalted by poets and tourist brochures. Every morning thousands leave those grim suburbs and head for the other Granada that the tourists visit. Hours later they can be seen on duty at the entrance to the *Alhambra*, selling souvenirs in the *cuesta Gomérez*, driving bus loads of tourists to the *Carthusian Monastery*, scrubbing the steps of the *Royal Chancellery* or showing someone the way to the

Campo del Príncipe. They are the gardeners, the cooks, the receptionists and general wardens of the ancient Granada.

In every city there are two cities: the historic city, preserved down the generations and dignified by time, and another, colourless, hidden city, whose most valuable possession is a throng of, anonymous men and women who can do the necessary jobs and carry out tasks skilfully. They are cities that share a name and are united by the work of these men and women. For the rest they are entirely unalike. When the old Granada empties at nightfall the new Granada comes to life; smells of spices and cooking waft through its windows mixed with snatches of dialogue from American films, and the lights stay on long after midnight. The builders working on the roof of the *Royal Chapel*, the gypsy women who offer carnations and read a happy future in the soft palms of nervous tourists, invariably full of health, children and dark-haired lovers (all for a token fee, although the token has a minimum set price of five hundred pesetas); the pensioners who congregate every day around a canary seller in *plaza Bibarrambla* to discuss the way prices never stop soaring and reminisce about their long-lost youth, when it rained more and in due season to boot, to complain about the disappearance of the public lavatories that used to be in the square before it was done up, all the while being photographed by Japanese tourists; the guides who explain the structure of the medieval *Elvira* city gate, point out the original course of the *Nasrid* fortified walls or praise the altarpiece in the monastery of *San Jerónimo*, the restaurant waitresses who serve the set menu to scuttling groups of boisterous tourists. All these are aliens in this historic part of the city, to which they come day after day with the same constancy and regularity as that with which they return on the *Day of the Dead* or the village's patron saint's day to the places they left years ago in search of a less humiliating future, where for a few hours they live once more in the houses they abandoned, renew the flowers in the niches in the cemetery, visit the relatives who either lacked the decisiveness or the strength to escape, stroll down streets invaded by nettles and given over to decay, just as on any Sunday in years gone by, while a peal of bells calls the faithful to mass in a village that no longer exists, peopled by ghosts who greet the ghosts they meet, all of them pretending that they aren't really ghosts at all.

Looking up into the night sky is a primitive, irrational act. It answers to neither rhyme nor reason. It is though, inevitable. We have no need to orient ourselves any more, nor do we have to calculate the time, or predict seasonal changes by the stars; all we have to do is to get onto a train, look at our watches and check with the calendar. Nevertheless, that vast silent realm has never ceased to fascinate us with the same mysterious power as it did our earliest ancestors. Although science has robbed the heavens of their mythology and no one nowadays believes in stories with celestial heroes, we haven't yet ceased to gaze at them speechless with wonder. At such moments one feels that nothing has changed for thousands of years, that when one asks oneself what those tiny brilliant points of light really mean one is engaged in an elemental rite, and one feels humbled by the mystery. At first sight the milky way is merely a conglomeration of imperturbable, brilliant dots of light, stars close to our sun, sailing in the middle of a space so immeasurably vast that we are incapable of imagining it. Although we perceive them as being fixed in a flat plane, the distances between them are enormous in all directions. The intensity of their light also varies. They are related in capricious patterns bearing Greek, Latin and Arabic names. Some of these stars by chance alone are sailing close to us, close enough for their individual light to reach us brightly. I can identify the seven stars of the *Great Bear*. They are not first-magnitude stars; two of them are called *Alcor* and *Mizar*. From there I know how to locate the pole star. I also recognise other surrounding constellations. It excites me to think that millions of eyes are looking at them at the same time as I am. The light of these stars has travelled millions of miles before we can see it. It takes so long to reach our eyes that the star which emitted the light and is now visible to us is not the same as it was then. Its image is not coetaneous with our sight. There were stars whose light was sent out towards us years, thousands of years ago, which have since disintegrated, although their glow, now without origin, continues travelling through space until some day they may become visible to us. Our eyes can only witness the universe's past, its irretrievable yesterday. When the image of a star reaches us the physiognomy of its origin has changed, be it ever so slightly, just as a man's face changes a tiny bit every day. What is present to our gaze is always past to the stars. We can only see the latest instant in a process of continuous mutability. Our today is in no way coeval with theirs; our present is their past, it forms part of the memory of the universe.

The lights that twinkle in the city appear to be whimsical constellations in the middle of an enormous shadowy field. When I look at Granada I see buildings being constructed, and theatres, prisons and schools that were finished years ago or were even born with the new century, and I also see two-hundred-year-old churches and fountains, and alongside them the city walls, the *Crimson Towers*, the *Arab baths*, the *Palace of Dar-al-Horra*, the *Convent of St. Isabel*, the *Royal Chancellery*, the *Royal Chapel*, vestiges of different ancient Granadas lent dignity by the centuries. Despite being built during very different periods they all now form part of the same present-day Granada. A city's present is an accumulation of its multiple, successive pasts. In looking at them we lend immediacy to the works of our ancestors. It is our own minds that break the city into fragments and establish its chronology. Granada is the outcome of many different cities, some lost, others still present today, of which only a part, and not the most important or final part, are the streets, the squares and the towers that we see today. Nothing is completely destroyed. The foundations of the new Granadas are built on the ruins of the old.

The columns of the primitive village *Iliberis* later went to support the roofs of Roman villas, whose marbles were in turn used to decorate the tombs of Arab cemeteries. The rubble from these was incorporated into the convents and palaces erected by the Christian conquerors, which inevitably fell down when their time came and were robbed for making theatres and gardens, used as spoil in the decoration of houses built of steel and glass. In *calle San Juan de los Reyes* there is a church built upon the devastated mosque of *Ateibín*, or *The Converted*, as it became known, because it belonged to Christians who had forsworn their religion.

On the personal command of *Queen Isabel I* its church was sanctified in the name of *St. John*, and thence the name of the street it stands in. It was the first church sanctified in the whole city after the conquest, probably as a lesson to the Christian renegades, but all the same the minaret of the mosque —designed, so local legend has it, in the thirteenth century by Sevillian builders in imitation of the *Giralda* in their own city— was spared and made into the tower of the new church. From that time onward the chiming of bells has replaced the wail of the muezzin, but the faithful are still being called to prayer from that same tower, originally built by believers in a different creed.

The tower of the parochial church of *San José* is another ancient minaret, which formed part of the mosque of *al-Murabitín*, or the "*Morabites*", upon the ruins of which the church was built. In one of its side walls there remains a horseshoe arch, which is probably one of the first of such design built in the whole city. The old courtyard of the principal mosque of the *Albaicín*, today forms the cloister of the church of *El Salvador,* often used by little girls as a playground to skip in while boys play football, using the arches of its colonnade as a goal. The residence of The *Admiral of Aragón, Don Francisco de Mendoza,* in the *Campo del Príncipe,* has seen use as an administrative building, a public hospital and a teacher-training college before becoming a military hospital, which in turn has only recently been closed. The convent of *Santa Cruz la Real,* which is now a student residence, has been in its day a museum, a school of fine arts, a barracks and a barn for drying tobacco. The church of *Perpetuo Socorro* was taken by French troops and converted into an arsenal and stable (the street running behind it retains this name) and later became a communal dwelling place, a refuge for the homeless and a charcoal warehouse. Hiding behind the walls of the convent of *Santa Catalina de Zafra* is a Moorish house and its baptismal font is the trough of a *Nasrid* fountain. The Christian *Corral del Carbón* was originally the Moorish *Alfondac Gidida,* a grain store and an inn and throughout the years has also served as a courtyard for travelling players, a communal residence and a bazaar. The church of *San Jerónimo* was built from stones taken from the Arabic city gate of *Elvira,* which was finally pulled down by the French three centuries later and the blocks used in the construction of the *Sebastiani* bridge over the *River Genil,* today known as the *Green Bridge.*

It is quite frequent in Granada to find a convent turned into a warehouse, a barracks, an hotel or a town hall, and a bank used at a later date as a church. The city is mutable, changing and adapting itself, and the stones provide the continuity for that one city, which, with its myriad faces, goes on calling itself Granada.

The fairness of a city derives from this coetaneous presence of all its pasts. Its splendour lies in its ability to fuse them all together. Uniformity and symmetry are fatal to it. What strengthens and dignifies a city is the interbreeding of generations, amalgamation and coexistence: what weakens and darkens it is waste, abandonment and the sly destruction of progress. Respect for its past lends a city nobility, whilst it is stunted by ignorance and greed, often disguised as fashion. A city's present is always ephemeral; scarcely has it begun to blossom when it becomes part of the past. Every tiny event of daily life alters it imperceptibly and nothing is as it was the minute before. At this moment an old man is painting the balcony of his house, some stoneworkers are paving a street with decorative cobbles, bulldozers are knocking down a mansion built at the end of the nineteenth century, a fountain is being transfered from one site to another, builders are repairing the tiles on a roof, a municipal gardener is watering the young trees in an as yet nameless square, a returned emigrant is renovating his old house with his life's savings; they are all altering the city's present and unconsciously building the past of those still to be born in Granada.

They come from every corner of the world, with exotic dress and cautious gait, their whole attention captured by a name: Granada. Beyond its bounds, way over the Pyrenees, on the far shores of the oceans, the very name conjures up the vision of a land blessed by nature and peopled by folk of genius. Tourists bring with them eyes accustomed to other skies, other countrysides and other faces. They walk through the city with the hesitation and wonder of a prisoner just freed from jail. They know they ought to capture something that they have come in search of but they are not quite sure what it might be. They stare at the passers by in the hope that they might find the answer in their faces. What is everyday for us is strange to them and by watching them observing us it is possible to discover things that familiarity has hidden from us: the gesticulations of the old men as they argue, the weird names over the doors of the undertakers', the atlantes and caryatids supporting the cornices of the balconies in the *Gran Vía*, the extravagant profusion in grocers' windows. Their ears too are sensitive to the wheeling cry of the swifts and the din of the market place. They are attracted to churches by the aroma of incense and to bars by the smell of frying cod. To write a letter they sit cross-legged resting the paper on their laps. They often stop and gaze upwards attentively in a way that clearly distinguishes them from the inhabitants, who hurry around apparently absorbed in the paving stones beneath their feet. Only the visitors spy the stone eagles perched on the banks, the angel with his fiery sword stretched out into space, guarding the streets below. Only they see the inscriptions and noble coats of arms emblazoned on lintels, the god surrounded by four mythical heroes who stand guard over the *Casa de los Tiros*, where the archives of the city are kept, the flaking signboards over repair shops for unheard-of typewriters, adding machines and cash registers, dilapidated names of lodging houses, whose past existence is only verified in old newspapers: *Central, Perales, Reina Isabel*, the empty niche in the wall dedicated to *Nuestra Señora del Buen Parto*, whose image has been replaced by one of an inopportune Nazarene Christ, and the splendid balconies, huge wooden structures encased in glass, with stone and iron balustrades, designed to see and be seen in, wide enough to help air the house but not so wide as to catch the full summer sun.

Granada is the name of a city made up of the innumerable and varied observations of travellers who have visited it over the centuries, the sum of which goes to build an extremely heterogeneous town, the city of those others, the strangers who have arrived down the years and registered in their pupils a dome here, a fountain there, a public garden, all of which they have taken back with them to the farthest extremes of the earth. And in this way Granada has been reconstructed with the bits and pieces acquired by every visitor during his visit: verbal accounts being added to word by word, a photograph, a trivial event, all augmenting the anonymous history of Granada, which was begun centuries ago, before this place came to be called Granada, or Garnata or even Ilíberis, and yet shepherds and wayfarers would stop to rest and admire it; a fluctuating and contradictory history which changes shape with every passing day and which circulates through the farthest reaches of both hemispheres and continues to grow with neither bounds nor discipline. Eyes accustomed to the monotony of sand and the desert horizon saw in Granada's abundance of fountains and irrigation channels, in the greenery of its fields, the realisation of their dreams. What for some are narrow, twisting, badly paved streets, are for others a delicious trace of oriental sensuality; where some see foul-smelling lodging houses offering even worse fare, others find the unrepeatable chance to meet exotic guests; the new buildings, lack-lustre and pointless to many, are also for some a sign of the city's vitality. Everyone speaks about the same city but not everyone has the same way of looking at it. A soldier may see with a different eye from that of a poet; an architect will not see the same things as a pedlar of bibles. But nevertheless, despite this diversity and

Albaicín.

Patio del Parador de San Francisco.

⇧ Patio de la Audiencia.

Patio de San Juan de Dios. ⇩

⬡ **Patio de la Cartuja.**

Patio del Colegio Mayor San Bartolomé y Santiago. ⬡

Patio de la Mezquita del Salvador.

Plaza Larga en El Albaicín (fiesta de la Cruz).

◁◁◁ **Plaza Nueva.**   ◁◁ **Un domingo en el Salón.**   ◁ **La Alcaicería.**   ⊟ **El Comercio.**   **Plaza Isabel la Católica.**

Interior de la Catedral. ⇦

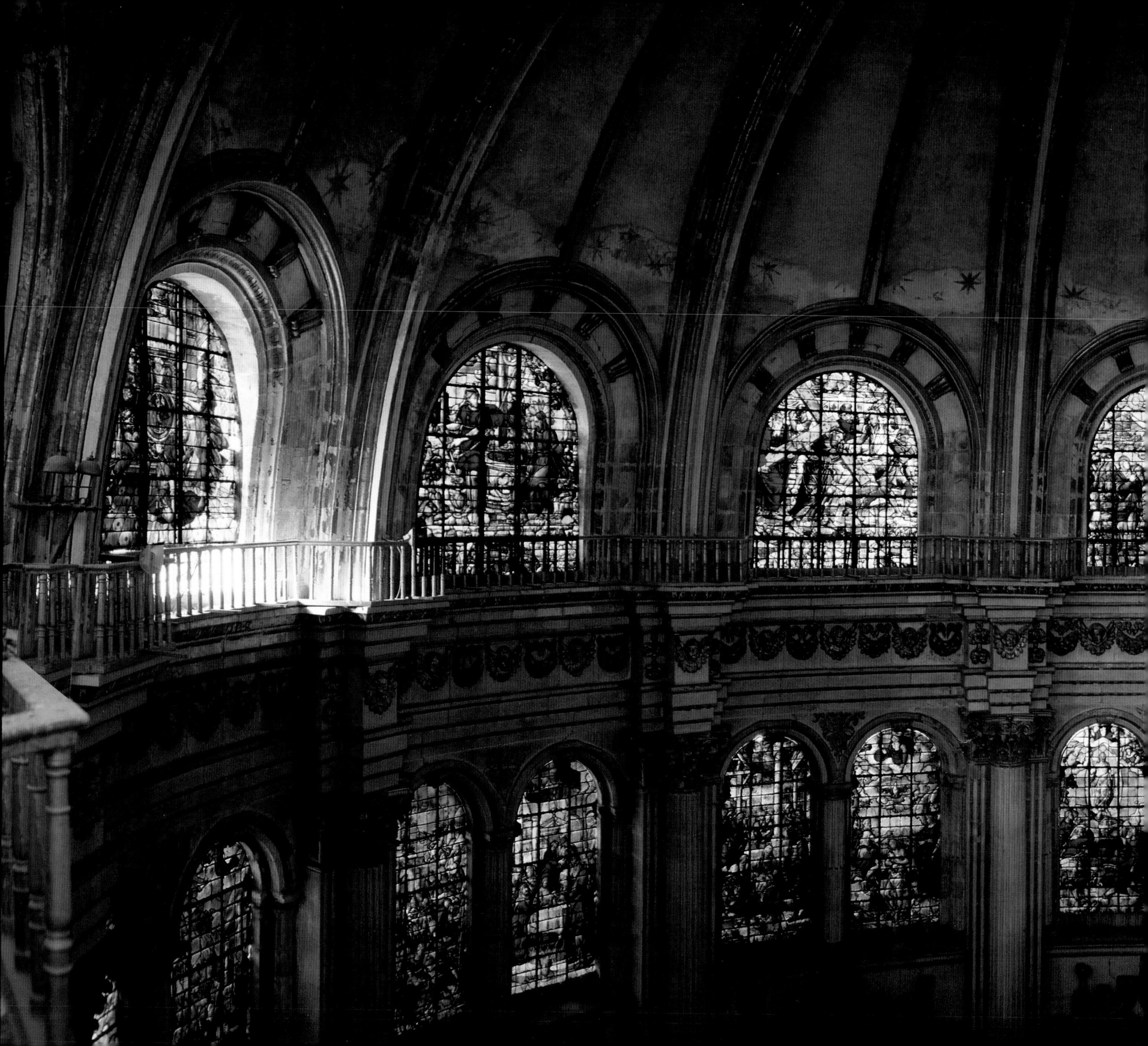

Vidrieras de la Capilla Mayor.

Campo del Príncipe.

⬆ **Plaza de San Nicolás.**

Plaza de Bib-Rambla. ⬇

⇦ **Procesión en el Campo del Príncipe.**   **Plaza de la Pescadería.** ⇨

◁◁ **Plaza de la Romanilla.** ◁ **Abadía del Sacromonte.** **Patio de San Jerónimo.** ◁ **Antigua Universidad.** ◁

Patio
(Carrera del Darro).

Patio del Albaicín.

Patio de los Córdova —31 de marzo de 1992— (llanto judío, 500 años de la Expulsión).

Colegio Notarial, patio.

Patio de la casa Janguas.

Patio del Albaicín.

Procesión de Sta. Mª de la Alhambra.

⇧ **Alhambra Palace.**

Tasca "Casa Enrique". ⇧

Palacio

Romería de San Miguel y Día de la Virgen.

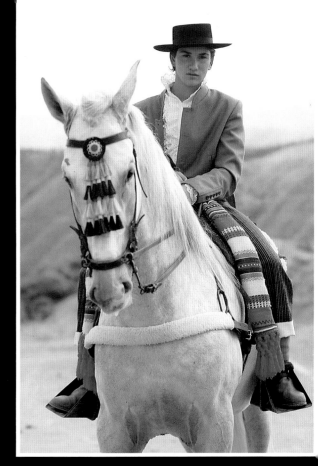

Romería de San Miguel y Día de la Virgen.

Bayárcal.

Páginas siguientes: Juviles y Bubión ◊   El Charcón ◊◊

Guadi

contrariness, —or perhaps because of it— the gaze of all of them has created the image of the city we call Granada and has imposed upon us a complex way of seeing and thinking about it.

Some of these travellers wrote about their experiences but others left scarcely any impression of themselves or of their passing. Of *General Horace Sebastiani*, commander of the French troops that occupied the city in 1810, who engineered the destruction of Granada with the same efficiency as he had earlier enhanced its beauty, we can only surmise a proud, lucid gaze, at once enlightened and intolerant. He pulled down convents and built theatres in their place; he spanned the river with bridges from the rubble of churches he had just flattened; and when he was ordered to withdraw from the city he had no compunction in blowing up the towers of the *Alhambra* he had just restored with such patience. Neither do we know what impression Granada had on *Malcolm Lowry*, that unkempt, chubby youth, who, a few days after arriving here in 1933, was acquainted with almost all the bars in the city and made the rounds of them daily with admirable punctuality, wearing a wide-brimmed hat which he considered *de rigueur* for an Andalucían buck. The kids called him "the English toper" and followed him around the streets making fun of him, imitating the stumbling, drunken antics of a young man soaked in cheap spirits. Slovenly and neurotic, he was living in the hostel *Carmona de Jan Gabrial*, enamoured of the woman who was to become his first wife and his bane, to whom he would recite passages of his unfinished novels on their walks through the gardens of the Generalife. Only years later, pursued by disaster and nightmare and fuelled by mescal and tequila, was he to complete in Cuernavaca his terrifying novel, "*Under the Volcano*", relating the irrevocable destiny of man, a veritable homage to the keenness of his vision. And in the verses of *San Juan de la Cruz*, such subtle descriptions of the mountains of the soul, we find perhaps the face of the city that he saw from his high vantage point in the *Campo de los Mártires*, from the courtyards of the monastery which he ministered to.

When I see the tourists standing in front of racks of postcards as though they were scrutinizing a display of fine jewellery, carefully choosing the pictures that conform most faithfully to their own perception of the city, I realise that history continues to run its course. Every postcard is one single fragment of Granada. Although they may have some elements in common —a rooftop, the ornamental grill on a window or some typical nook— collected together into sets they create different cities. One such city has high, stone façades and wide avenues full of traffic, whilst in another there are no cars to be seen; the markets are reached through steep, crowded, narrow streets, the houses are walled in, allowing glimpses of palm trees, cypresses and grape vines. The tourists buy their postcards and take an illusory city away with them in a white envelope, an exclusive collection of images shuffled at random, but they all nevertheless call these images Granada and when they get home they show their friends the town they have just visited. Thus the Granada they talk about in Zaragoza might be full of little white houses crowded together and has a river running through it spanned by stone bridges. This view of Granada may not be the one shared by the inhabitants of Stockholm, where they think of Moorish palaces, the painted stucco of public bathhouses and gardens. The Granada shown across the table in Tokyo, on the other hand, has no cars, the only means of locomotion being trains of donkeys wearing straw hats; the women all have long raven hair and defiant eyes and the men play guitars at the entrances to caves in the *Sacromonte*. These are all cities invented by eyes unshrouded by boredom or routine, eyes open to novelty and surprise.

A city contains as many cities as it has visitors. Cities only exist within us and we look beyond ourselves for visual confirmation of an image we already have inside us. When we look at Granada's streets and windows, swallows' nests in the eaves, a wall ulcerated like the face of a leper, dark-eyed girls leaning over balconies, rubbish strewn around at street corners, we are really looking at that interior vision. Everything exists as a mirror image of our own city. All of the possible Granadas reside in each of us. I realise full well, however, that throughout my life I shall only know one city, invisible to everyone else. And when I speak of Granada I shall perhaps be speaking about a city which only exists in the winding pathways of my own memory.

At one end of the narrow, derelict *calle Elvira*, part of one of the main gates in the *Nasrid* city walls still stands. This street forms the southern boundary to the *Albaicín* quarter. Many side streets run down into it from the hill quarter which was once occupied by an Arab military cast, the *Zenetes*. If you look at the vestiges of earlier ages dotted along this street — chapels, stone lintels, coats of arms, fountains and drinking troughs— it is not difficult to imagine a past less blighted than today. It was a street conceived for mules and carts, but nowadays even the pavements are blocked with cars and it is no longer an agreeable experience to stroll along it. It is lined houses which only remain standing by a miracle, their walls eaten away and leached of all colour, held together by ancient filth, roofs sodden and gutters rotten with age and choked with weeds. They would seem at first glance to be abandoned (a few are in fact), but clothes strung out to dry on their narrow balconies, which are also usually full of household bric-à-brac and pot plants covered with sheets of plastic, blinds as tatty as the houses themselves rolled down over the verandas, all betray signs of life going on in the midst of this first external impression of desolation. The houses are interspersed with waste lots blocked off with low, crumbling walls and infested with old furniture and flea-ridden mattresses, weeds, building rubble and household rubbish, and presided over by prosperous colonies of cats. Oid wine cellars, such as the *Bodega Castañeda,* are a reminder of the days when you got drunk for a reason and took time and patience over it. Ancient shops still with counters and shop keepers behind them have grown old along with their proprietors. On the flaking walls modern graffiti share space with old sign boards which recall an age that progress has rapidly converted into legend: *Charcoal Store San Antonio,* or *Residence Pilar del Toro.* This latter name, carved into the stone lintel of a town mansion with huge knockers on double doors, wide enough to open up and admit a carriage, marks the original site of the fountain and trough carved by *Diego de Siloé,* since

moved to the nearby *plaza de Santa Ana.* Ruin abounds, and, sadly, the more so the nearer you get to the old Arab gate.

All the town's junk shops are collected in this street, old furniture, antique bazaars. Their windows are a hymn of praise to all that is old: cast-iron bedsteads, plinths of pillars, marquetry boxes, hand-carved cedar cabinets, statues of saints, fonts for holy water, porcelain teapots, silver candelabras, jewel boxes inlaid with mother-of-pearl, and brass mortars. This juxtaposition of ruin and splendour is somehow offensive; how it jars, the contrast between the degraded antiquity of the street and venerated antiquity inside the shops. Perhaps though this display of the cinders and ashes of its own past all jumbled up together shows the city as it really is. Only the sight of the street´s decay allows us to put a real value on what has been preserved; or else, the glorification of the small and fragmentary treasures inside shows up the penury of their surroundings. Some understanding of Granada may come forth from that apparently contradictory alliance of abandoned buildings and grimy walls, and shelves full of porcelain and cameos. We are irresistibly drawn to the old. Perhaps in order not to forget the comprehensible elements of our lives. Without knowing why, we shun the wide avenues and allow our feet to stray towards the empty, shady, narrow alleyways where children swap comics on doorsteps, cabinet makers and locksmiths are absorbed in their exacting crafts, and the noise of family squabbles and guffaws of laughter escapes from windows all around. New, unusual things of modern design fascinate us but we find solace in objects which are old and worn out. We are involved in a constant tug-of-war between the newly born and what has passed on. We invent new things but we cannot do without the old. When we travel to visit unknown towns it is to see its old things, its relics and remains.

The centuries have piled up their work in Granada with scarcely any effort. We are comforted by the security of decaying constructions, the patina that time has deposited on walls, the worn-down edges of steps, which give us the sensation of being mere participants in a centuries-old process that will not come to an end with us. These things rid us of the anxiety and uncertainty caused by the unknown, the unease and disorder which new things awaken in us. Those old, ruinous, apparently abandoned houses, damp, grimy, cracked and flaking, whose only hint of life persevering inside them is in the washing hung out and the pots of geraniums on the balconies, make cities different in something more than in name. They make the city seem more approachable, less unknown and more human.

Looking into the windows of antique shops is like peering curiously and indiscreetly into a house whose window has been absent-mindedly left ajar. The temptation to look in is irresistible; we are all nosy little leprechauns at heart. Furniture and domestic odds and ends are lying around as though on the eve of a house moving. I like the disorder and the absence of modern devices, the anachronous silence of that room in contrast to the din in the street, where motorbikes with cut-off exhausts roar up and down, where the gas delivery men announce their arrival by crashing the bottles together on the lorry and cars hoot at the slightest delay. Looking into the shop window I find it easy to imagine the interior of a room, to arrange the furniture and knick-knacks on sale according to my whim, to recompose a world long gone: the white lace curtains drawn back from a window; the portrait of a stern-faced gentleman with a patriarch's moustache presiding over a wall full of family photographs, tiny portraits and ceramic plates; a dresser set like an altar; a wooden case with the statue of a saint taking pride of place in the centre and around it a small light burning, photograph frames, a vase of flowers and reliquaries; a mirror with bevelled edges; an upright piano in a corner; a lamp with pendant teardrop crystals; a bedside table skirted with velvet and topped with a little embroidered linen mat; a three-piece suite upholstered in damask with a copy of "Cosmopolitan" laid out upon it; some shelves holding leather-bound books. I also allow myself to imagine that the black-and-white-tiled floor is recently scrubbed and that a tune from a gramophone can be heard from beyond a door leading to the hallway. And then I include in the scene moments of boredom, secret confidences, instructions being given, parties, gliding shadows on the other side of the hall. Almost certainly the people who once bought the furniture piled up in the shop and used it for a lifetime, taking it with them whenever they moved house, are dead now and their belongings await other hands to touch them and other homes to grow old in.

A city is also the life that goes on inside rooms. Many claim that the real Granada is hiding in those private places. For this reason it has been said that it is a hermetic city, secret and absorbed in itself, enamoured of the small and intimate things in life, given to seclusion. It is really a blending of different traditions, the cloister of the convent and the oriental harem; Castillian asceticism, which voluntarily renounces pleasure in glory, and Moorish modesty, which hides the most delicate of gardens behind fortified walls. Its spirit is that which manifests itself essentially in these enclosed paradises, which poets have sung of and have woven into a metaphor of the city. The very essence of Granada is the *carmen*, a house surrounded by a walled garden full of cypresses and palm trees, orange and lemon blossom, myrtles and wisteria, jasmine that flows over and cascades into the street; in the centre an old stone fountain, its rim worn smooth by time, a pergola beneath a trellised grape vine, a tessellated pebble floor depicting animals, now grown over with moss, an orchard forbidden to outside eyes, fenced in with jalousies and bolted from within.

We see only the outside of buildings in cities. The image they leave in our memories comes mainly from their façades. They are superficial cities. We claim to know a town because we have strolled down its streets and seen towers, friezes, verandahs, murals and door knockers. But we have never crossed the threshold of a single house; we know nothing of the laughter inside them, the confidential secrets told over the phone, the gestures of girls in front of a glass, the way that the diners are sat. We are aware that stories about the adventures and obsessions of ordinary men and women are intimately tied to insignificant, personal objects. The passions, desires, petty personal ambitions of those who go to create the invisible Granada by their mere presence in it are all contained in a diary, a letter, a paperweight, a watch, a jewellery case, a musical box, a photograph album or a key.

Attempting to understand the very essence of a city, to capture it in words is a desperate quest. In vain we try to crystallize it just as we cling to the last fleeting images of a dream on waking. Some grasp it in the firm, immutable city that belongs to generation after generation; others guess at it in what is about to disappear, in the changeable and ephemeral. Some see it in the flux of the street, others in what happens in rooms behind closed doors. It is a fruitless temptation, a task akin to that of Tantalus. There comes a moment in our lives when the quiet pleasure of knowing replaces the urge to interpret, and judgment is no longer so important as the recognition of truth. The city is one and many at the same time. It is concentrated into a golden cameo showing the profile of a woman in mother of pearl, and it is also the *Elvira Gate* lovingly restored to commemorate the five-hundredth anniversary of the subjugation of the Moors in Granada.

From the pavement outside I can only see the narrow porch —its floor covered in filth and the litter that the wind has blown through the iron grill— and the little window where we bought our tickets, so low that we had to bow down to it; two empty glass-fronted cases, broken now, with a notice saying SHOWING TODAY above them. The entrance is dark and what lies beyond can only be imagined: the foyer where we waited impatiently for the film to start; the swing doors we jostled through into the auditorium, the steep steps leading up to the back rows, the curtain that hid the screen before the programme began. The auditorium must be pitch dark now, full of dust and cobwebs and overrun with rats, its seats torn, the whole place as sad as an abandoned communal courtyard that once harboured dozens of chattering families. We have almost got used to that ruined shell and pass it by as though we had never been inside, as though we had never enjoyed our outings to the pictures and the place was a slum to be avoided, as though we had never in days gone by stopped on our way down *calle Puentezuelas* to look at what was on, blocking the pavement while we looked at the stills in their glass cases to decide whether the film was worth seeing or not.

When one stops now to look at the pitiful state of the *Goya* cinema one realises that nostalgia is nothing abnormal, nor is it a wasteful emotion; it is in fact an expression of will, a defence against forgetting the places where one knew a certain degree of happiness. A derelict cinema does not leave me indifferent, any more than does the closure of a library or the disappearance of a public square; they are all places which have been essential parts of our apprenticeship in life. One cannot remain unmoved to see the cinemas of one's youth turned into blocks of flats, furniture factories, supermarkets, entertainment halls; or even left deserted, like the four empty, ghostly cinemas that I see every day with mounting irritation. This decay and destruction is an attack upon the most unsullied realms of the memory. One has left far too many hours of one's life in those now filthy, unoccupied cinemas, sitting in silence, in sole possession of the faces, the gestures and the voices of the actors, to accept that their extinction should be one more simple episode in the life of the city, something apart from our life's history, at least from our insubstantial identity as spectators. Our experiences of the city are inseparable from the experiences we have lived through at the cinema. They are interwoven: we learnt to see the city more clearly because the cinema taught us to observe, in the same way that the eyes which watched films had been educated by the lights and the real characters walking abroad in the city. The streets which had lead irresistibly to the cinema a couple of hours earlier, on leaving had become a mediocre reflection of the imaginary ones we had just seen on the screen.

In one of these cinemas I would often come across a blind man, whose presence perturbed me somewhat. It seemed to me unreasonable, illogical. I couldn't comprehend the interest he showed in films. Such apparently incongruous behaviour does not disturb me so much now. I have learnt about the power of words. In those days, on the occasions we coincided there, his dark gaze affected mine and I couldn't stop looking across at him during the film, studying his fixed expression, looking for any reaction he might show, wondering at the way he seemed to be completely immersed in the unfathomable world conjured up by the music and dialogue of the film. Only when he discerned that the film was ending did he relax his solemn pose. Without more ado and with the same natural ease with which he had taken his seat near the exit he would leave the auditorium. Sometimes I saw that someone was waiting for him at the entrance and they would both vanish silently into the surrounding streets. One day he stopped coming. Or maybe his absence coincided with the closing of the cinema. From time to time I have asked myself how that unusual cinema goer would have reacted if one day he had regained his sight, whether he could have borne the faces of the actors whom had he had imagined through the quality of their voices alone. Perhaps not. Beyond his obscure world it would probably have been difficult for him to come to terms with reality; it would have seemed shabby compared to the world conjured up by the voices of the actors.

In 1976 *Jorge Luis Borges* visited the *Alhambra*. I can imagine him walking cautiously, holding tightly onto the arm of *María Kodama*, listening silently and intently to her explanations, nodding in agreement from time to time, staring fixedly in front of him as she pointed out inscriptions along the walls. Later he wrote a poem to commemorate his visit, in which he praises the murmur of its flowing waters, the softness of its marble, the scent of jasmine and the stories his companions had told him about it. The *Alhambra* which he was unable to see was for him a concert of sounds and textures, smells, words and sensations with which to create a palace of beauty. Whenever I find myself in the *Alhambra* that poem always comes to mind.

I see groups of tourists trickle into the palaces and the gardens with the same unruly curiosity that the Christian troops must have shown in those turbulent days in January 1492 when they first broke into the fortified palatial city that they had seen so often glowing with light in the distance during weary, red-eyed nights on guard. They must have felt desire tempered by a certain fear of the fame of this irreducible bastion, their imaginations fevered by the fantastic tales that ran from mouth to mouth in the besieging camps and surrounding towns, which rumoured that the stone fortress hid a palace with walls of silk brocade, floors tiled with marble as white as ass's milk, gardens so vast that a hermit could live secluded in them and never be disturbed and that the sound of water running from the countless fountains in them was never still. Such fame was spread by ambassadors, captives and muleteers alike, people whose accounts could be trusted as they had succeeded in reaching the very outskirts of those sealed precincts and had returned struck with wonder. Some time later the members of the royal embassy were to cross the *River Genil* and climb the deserted southern slope of the *Alijares* hill to possess the fortress whose keys had just been handed over to them; and they as well scoured around it with the same sense of amazement and intimidation. The new conquerors arriving from all over the world must share similar feelings when they filter through the timeless labyrinth of corridors, halls and courtyards, whose names they will never remember, cast their eyes over the seemingly unreal tiles running around the walls, the multicoloured plasterwork of the vaulted ceilings, the delicate marquetry of the doors. They climb and descend in orderly file, endlessly photographing and milling around surrounded by the same confusion and bustle that I imagine must have followed the conquest of the city, when, the original fears of an ambush or an uprising having been laid to rest, *King Ferdinand* and *Queen Isabel* left their camp at *Santa Fé* and installed themselves in the

Alhambra. I can picture the distant hustle and bustle, the carrying of furniture and curtains, the greedy lingering of the new lords of the city over the abandoned spoils, books left open on reading desks, tables covered in fabrics and necklaces; I can hear the laughter of the servants carrying cabinets and chests, spreading out carpets and curtains and piling up in corners earthenware and banners discarded by the vanquished. I can imagine all that tumult when I look at today's invaders, swarming everywhere like a colony of ants, afraid they might be the victims of some great elaborate hoax, urged on by their guides, tracing the inscriptions on the walls with their fingers, stroking the doors, leaning precipitouslly out of the miradors, constantly looking at their watches, determined to see everything, to keep to schedule, not to be late for lunch. They lean giddily out of windows to point out some landmark on the horizon, a weather vane, a crane, a column of smoke and they feel as though they were lords of the city spread out below them, as though they had just conquered it, inflamed like the first Christian soldiers who hoisted the cross and the banner of Castille over this fortress on the day they occupied it. They were Basques, Aragonese, Asturians, Galicians and Castllians, all born in far-flung parts, who suddenly found themselves guarding gates with unpronounceable names, patrolling gloomy parapets during long nights on duty, watching the strangely uniform white houses of the *Albaicín* across the river, with its crown of minarets, hearing snatches of conversations in unintelligible tongues born on the wind together with the smells of unknown herbs and stews; a citadel thrice encircled by fortified walls like copper bracelets, traces of which can still be made out from the *Tower of Comares.*

Visitors stare at the tiles with the same intense concentration that you see in the eyes of drunks or lunatics, but it isn't enough to just look, even with the widest of eyes. Something more is needed. It isn't sufficient to believe that they are beautiful, unrepeatable and unique. You have to submit to the mystery of the enigma. Looking without understanding is tantamount to admitting to a crass ineptitude, the inability to see through mere appearances to decipher the principles behind the intertwining tracery of the friezes, the combinations of colours; religious beliefs expressed in the language of geometry. The only way is to reach beyond fascination alone and divine the hidden wisdom of the designers of these mosaics, see into the workshops where their ideas were drawn, imagine the tables strewn with papers and geometrical instruments, meticulous mathematical calculations which brought the concepts to life. These mosaics are the culmination of a thousand years of wisdom and strict mathematical discipline. But the tourists are unaware of the rules behind them, neither are they familiar with the alphabet which the inscriptions and poems running around the walls of the *Hall of the Ambassadors* are written in, signs that perhaps contain the description of a garden, a hymn of praise, a prayer, a lament, or a single word to define the whole world.

The *Alhambra* has been seen by thousands of eyes but not all have seen the same thing. What did the original occupants see there? What did the infidels see when they occupied it in 1492? What have the innumerable visitors to the palace seen since that time? What do those hurried tourists with their cameras slung round their necks really see? What in fact do I see? I certainly do not see what they were able to contemplate when the palace was at the apotheosis of its splendour. We don't see anything like an intact structure today. We can only see a shadow of what was. The *Alhambra* is as fragile as a cobweb that has miraculously resisted the onslaught of the centuries: catastrophes, war, despoliation and ill-advised patching up, all of which have been disfiguring its face since the first days of the conquest. Systematic theft from the structure has been a routine occurrence. *Gustave Doré* has left us an unforgettable description of the tile robber, a predator with a taste for art who was working until quite recently. The *Alhambra*

has been left to decay into a miserable ruin, a stopover for muleteers, a crowded tenement, where poor families held their wild and noisy get-togethers, drunks sprawled out, and mothers washed their children in the ornamental lakes and fountains in patios now zealously guarded and protected. Its cellars have been used as dungeons, its towers as gunpowder stores, the vaults of its bath houses were for centuries the natural roost of bats. Its halls were magnificent stables for privileged donkeys. There was a time when anyone could go and take over part of the buildings for his own use, maybe to pass the hot summer months. *Washington Irving* tells how during his stay in the *Alhambra* an ageing count arrived one day and expropriated the *Salón de los Ambajadores* to stay in during a shooting holiday he had planned in the area, and that they divided up their respective territories without the slightest rancour, the *Patio de los Leones* for one and the *baths* and *Lindaraja gardens* for the other. For several years the great halls served as barracks for the occupying French troops, who, having spent considerable time and effort on repairing parts of the palace, nevertheless blew up several of its towers when they were forced to withdraw from the city. It has also been a hideout for smugglers and rogues of all kinds, while at the same time visitors to the city have been able to climb the hill and wander freely around its towers, halls and grounds.

We are seduced by the charms of the *Alhambra* but we still fail to understand the cunning of its layout; its structure is an alphabet which is unintelligible to our eyes. We see open spaces, artificial lakes, columns, walls tiled with interlaced patterns, scalloped plasterwork and subtly designed adornments everywhere we look, but we are unable to comprehend the splendid marriage of fantasy and discipline that they represent. The precision of a theorem is placed in perfect unison with the delicate perfection of a poem. Despite the admiration which its splendour excites in us, or perhaps because of it, the *Alhambra* has never really given up the secret of its true identity to us. We know almost nothing about it despite the years we have spent looking at it. We are all blind. Neither am I at all sure that the city we have come to know with our eyes wide open is the truest or the most complete one. The city which we have looked at so often is not the only one nor is it the best of all its possible identities. The boundary separating the real city from another imaginary one is as tenuous as the blink of an eyelid.

From the bus I have witnessed the *Palacio de Congresos* rising skyward, watched how the builders have shaped it, covered it pompously in green marble imported from Guatemala. And for a few minutes every day I share the journey with students sitting beside me on their way to and from school, noisy and gregarious, self-assured in their youth, exchanging jokes and banal, second-hand observations picked up along the way. We look at the same sight from the bus windows, at a construction that their eyes as well as mine have been getting used to over the months. But how differently we see it! They, just as free from any obligation as they are from nostalgia, think that it is tremendous, "*Mega*" and "*Brobdignagian*", they call it. Their memories are being built at the same time as the congress centre itself. I, on the other hand, can't stand the sight of it, neither its architectural design, nor its opulence, nor its astronomical cost, nor its very existence. This building is stealing from me a space in my memory that was taken up by other things. *The Paseo del Violón* was not always the avenue I see today from the bus. But it demands more and more effort of me to conjure up the memory of its old face. As a defence against forgetfulness I have deliberately brought to mind every detail of how it used to be —the wall that surrounded the forbidden precinct of the *Royal Tennis Society* and the waste-ground that was left when it disappeared, where gypsies camped with their grubby caravans, canvas tents and broken-down old cars. I have recalled events— games, races, the sweat of a time when the ground now occupied by blocks of flats, hotels and fire stations was a spacious school stadium for young athletes to train in. When from time to time our ball went over the wall into the narrow, deserted alley beyond and no one was passing by to answers our calls; we had to leave the school and look for it, hoping as we ran round that no one had pinched it in the meantime. Above all it brings back memories of the fairground, when "hell's alley" ran from the bridge over the *River Geníl* to the hermitage of *San Sebastián*, a primitive Moslem marabout, and to the *Alcázar Geníl*, the pleasure palace built for *King Boabdil's* mother: the Ferris wheel, the roundabouts, the big dipper, the ghost train, the Giant American Circus, Manolita Chen's Chinese Circus, shooting galleries, the serpent woman, the hall of mirrors, the tombola, the air redolent with the smell of kebabs and hot cooking oil, the candy-floss stalls, attractions that arrived on time every year like migrating birds for the festival of *Corpus Christi* in this very avenue.

I have propped these memories about me in self defence. This city that is growing up before my eyes, the city that will define the face of Granada in the future —the sports stadium, the ring-road, the science estate, the park dedicated to *Federico García Lorca*— have all been constructed over land that I once trod; they overlap with an intimate Granada which grew as I did. Memories

are very ephemeral but they can be shored up and made firm. I realised that my memories were of another city which was receding further and further into the past and with the ferocity of a mother lion I had to preserve them from the attack of the new city, the Granada that the adolescents beside me on the bus considered theirs and would in their turn defend in later life from the Granadas yet to come. The *Gran Via de Colón* is not just a wide avenue lined with ostentatious administrative buildings; it is also the memory of an old Moslem mosque knocked down to provide easy access from the city centre to the brand new railway station and a reminder of the economic euphoria which accompanied the planting of sugar beet and the construction of sugar mills in the plains around the city —now empty, spectral ruins like scenes from a Gothic novel— , a monument to the architects who traced its line and the grief of the inhabitants evicted from their old houses. But all these events have been forgotten and we are only left with stairways, entrance foyers, intricately worked barred windows, balconies with elegantly carved supports, and domes. I am aware that when these new constructions have finally been incorporated into the consciousness of the population and have even become objects of veneration, such as the *Royal Chapel* or the church of *San Juan de Dios* are to us, the city that I believed to be the real one will have disappeared for good. The shapes of the streets and some stone will remain but the ideas and controversies behind it all will have dissolved and vanished. A few photographs, a couple of pictures and some memories will be all that survive for a while.

Other people with other sentiments will later be attached to these new buildings and upon these they will construct their own life stories. The village boy, who arrived in a city called Granada like a survivor from a shipwreck cast up upon a deserted shore, both ignorant and wholly dependent on fortune, learned here to look and understand. We do not all walk through the past in the same way nor down the same streets. Every city imposes its own rules and its own limits on us. And there comes a time when the history of a city is part of one's own personal past. Suddenly one is aware that Granada is the name of a realm in one's memory. One can no longer conceive of the things belonging to this city as apart from one's own existence. They concern one and are precious because one's memories are constructed around them. The city which I arrived in with neither awareness nor aspirations no longer exists. Its common past, which at first was unknown and irrelevant to me, has since changed. Without being aware of it my own past has merged into that of the city.